BY REQUEST

Most Wanted Recipes from Arizona's Favorite Restaurants

BETSY MANN

NORTHLAND PUBLISHING

For Dinn and Caroline, my expert taste-testers.

The text type was set in Minion
The display type was set in Minion Display Italic
Composed and manufactured in the United States of America
Art director: Jennifer Schaber
Designer: Trina Stahl
Editor: Heath Lynn Silberfeld
Editorial supervision by Stephanie Bucholz
Production supervision by Lisa Brownfield

NOTES: All cooking temperatures in this book refer to the Fahrenheit scale.
Where serving sizes vary, nutritional values are based on the larger serving size unless otherwise
noted, e.g., 4 servings for recipes that serve 4 to 6. All parts of the recipe—dressings, dips, etc.—
are included in the nutritional values unless these are provided separately.
The use of trade names does not imply an endorsement by the product manufacturer.

FIRST IMPRESSION
ISBN 0-87358-730-8

Library of Congress Catalog Card Number 98-3982
Cataloging-in-Publication Data
Mann, Betsy, date.
By request : most wanted recipes from Arizona's favorite
restaurants / Betsy Mann.
p. cm.
Includes bibliographical references and index.
ISBN 0-87358-730-8
1. Cookery—Arizona. 2. Restaurants—Arizona—Guidebooks.
I. Title.
TX715.M276 1998
641.59791—dc21   98-3982

700/5M/9-98

Contents

ACKNOWLEDGMENTS

I gratefully extend my thanks to Judy Walker for her constant support and professional advice throughout the years, and the rest of the "Food!" staff at *The Arizona Republic*. I also appreciate the support of Erin Murphy and Stephanie Bucholz of Northland Publishing for bringing this dream of mine to reality. Thanks go especially to my husband Dinn for his patience and willingness to taste my burnt bread pudding, and to the readers who take the time to write such warm letters requesting these fabulous recipes.

My deepest gratitude also goes to all the chefs, bakers, owners, and managers who took time from their busy schedules to share their recipes with you and me.

INTRODUCTION

ARIZONA OFFERS SO MUCH BEAUTY, so much in the way of breathtaking sights. More than any other characteristic, though, Southwestern cuisine is the slice of Arizona that can, literally, be cooked up anywhere.

Peppers. Sweets. Cheeses. Breads.

From the Valley of the Sun to Tucson, from Prescott to Sedona, and from countless other desert dots on the map, I have enjoyed the privilege of seeking out the secrets that make Arizona restaurants irresistible. Four years ago, the *Arizona Republic* gave me the opportunity to try my power of persuasion on the artists/chefs who prepare much of the area's remarkable foods. Making the task more rewarding was the fact that every recipe acquisition for "By Request," a weekly feature in the *Republic,* has started with a simple, impassioned note from people a lot like you.

Now, wherever I am, these requests keep me connected to the people and the places that make up the extraordinary tastes of Arizona. Each week, I get about twenty pleas from Grand Canyon State residents, including snowbirds and others who crave the chance to recreate restaurant dishes at home. This book is a compilation of 102 recipe requests that various chefs graciously answered.

The best time for me is when the aroma from a recipe fills my family's home with scents from an unforgettable establishment's creative kitchen.

Yum!

My husband suggested we make this a scratch-and-sniff book, which got me thinking. In many ways, it already is. The ingredients alone give away a certain savory sensation that is sure to make your taste buds twitch.

Poblanos. Chipotles. Warm tortillas. Flan. Bread puddings. Cilantro.

See what I mean?

What's more, because Arizona has such delightful variety, these recipes aren't restricted to Southwestern-style foods. Inside, you'll find salads, soups, and side dishes to accompany main dishes and desserts for any number of appetites.

Think of this book as a giant menu, one that was created by popular demand for people who adore Arizona and all it has to offer—including the many generous establishments and thousands of letter writers who make my work enormously rewarding.

APPETIZERS

BAKED GOAT CHEESE

Cucina! Cucina! Italian Cafe

PARADISE VALLEY, AHWATUKEE,
AND PHOENIX, ARIZONA

John Nye, Corporate Executive Chef

THIS UNIQUE APPETIZER will keep people coming back for more. Baked goat cheese—covered with bread crumbs and chopped pine nuts and spread on baguette slices (crostini)—is a superb prelude to any meal.

3 ounces goat cheese (about ¾ cup)
2 tablespoons fine bread crumbs
2 teaspoons pine nuts, chopped
4 tablespoons plus ½ tablespoon extra-virgin olive oil
2 cloves garlic, minced
1 baguette

Form goat cheese into a 3-inch disk. In a small dish combine bread crumbs and chopped pine nuts, then pat mixture evenly onto goat cheese disk and set aside.

Heat 4 tablespoons of the olive oil in a small sauté pan over medium-low heat. Add garlic and caramelize slowly for about 15 to 20 minutes until it changes color to a light golden brown. Remove garlic and set aside, reserving the oil.

Preheat oven to 300 degrees.

To make crostini, slice baguette at an angle in ¼-inch-thick pieces about 4 inches long. Brush both sides of each bread slice with the reserved olive oil. Place the crostini on a cookie sheet and bake for 20 minutes, or until light brown. Remove from oven and let cool to room temperature.

Increase oven temperature to 450 degrees and place goat cheese on a cookie sheet. Bake for 3 to 4 minutes, or until bread crumbs turn a light golden color and cheese begins to puff. Sprinkle caramelized garlic over baked goat cheese and drizzle remaining ½ tablespoon olive oil on top. Serve on a large plate surrounded by crostini.

MAKES 6 APPETIZER SERVINGS

Approximate values per serving: 162 calories, 8 grams fat, 15 milligrams cholesterol, 16 grams carbohydrate, 7 grams protein, 222 milligrams sodium, 42 percent of calories from fat.

SAM'S BREADSTICKS

Sam's Cafe

PHOENIX AND SCOTTSDALE, ARIZONA

Tudie Frank Johnson, Corporate Chef

THESE POPPY SEED BREADSTICKS make an exceptional appe tizer, especially when served with Spicy Cream Cheese Dip. You'll be surprised to find how easy it is to make such a delicious dip. Great for unexpected company.

1½ teaspoons rapid-rise yeast
1 tablespoon sugar
1½ teaspoons olive oil
½ cup warm water
1 teaspoon garlic salt
1½ cups bread flour
Parchment paper to line sheet pan
½ teaspoon cornmeal
1 egg

2 tablespoons milk

1 to 2 tablespoons poppy seeds

Spicy Cream Cheese Dip (recipe follows)

In a large mixing bowl, combine yeast, sugar, oil, and water. Mix well and let sit 5 minutes to start yeast.

With an electric mixer set on low speed, add garlic salt and flour in batches. When incorporated, the dough should be a ball moving around the bowl. Let dough knead in mixer on medium speed for 4 to 5 minutes, or knead by hand on a lightly floured surface.

Remove dough to a flour-dusted surface and pat out to 1 inch thick. Let rest 10 minutes.

Heat oven to 415 degrees.

Cut dough into 2 to 3 pieces, each about 4 inches wide. Cut these pieces across into 1-inch-wide strips. Roll out into sticks about ½ inch thick and 8 inches long.

Line a sheet pan with parchment paper and dust with cornmeal. Space breadsticks about 1 inch apart. Lightly beat egg and milk together. Brush breadsticks with egg wash and sprinkle with poppy seeds. Bake for 6 to 7 minutes until soft and golden.

SERVES 12

SPICY CREAM CHEESE DIP

16 ounces cream cheese

½ cup medium picante sauce

Place cream cheese in a small mixing bowl and mix about 5 minutes on low speed until fluffy, scraping the sides and bottom. Add picante sauce and mix until incorporated. Refrigerate until ready to use.

MAKES 4 CUPS

Approximate values per serving (one breadstick with 1 tablespoon of dip): 141 calories, 7 grams fat, 33 milligrams cholesterol, 14 grams carbohydrate, 59 milligrams sodium, 45 percent of calories from fat.

BLACK BEAN HUMMUS

Old Town Tortilla Factory
SCOTTSDALE, ARIZONA

Patrick Hughes, Chef

THIS IS ONE OF THE BEST appetizers in the Valley, according to many Phoenix residents. Try it once and you'll be sold.

1 cup black beans, fully cooked
2 large cloves roasted garlic
¼ cup chopped fresh cilantro
⅓ cup fresh lime juice
½ teaspoon toasted cumin seeds, crushed
1 tablespoon kosher salt
¾ teaspoon black pepper
⅓ cup tahini paste
⅓ cup water
1 tablespoon balsamic vinegar

In a blender or food processor, combine all ingredients. Purée until smooth.

Serve with chips and salsa.

MAKES 4 CUPS

NOTE: *Tahini paste is a creamy purée of sesame seeds that has a light, nutlike flavor. It is widely used in Latin American cooking and can be found in well-stocked grocery stores.*

To roast garlic, cut ½ inch off the top of a whole garlic bulb, exposing clove tops. Remove loose outer skin, leaving bulb intact. Place on a piece of aluminum foil and drizzle with about 1 tablespoon of olive oil. Wrap in foil and place in a 450-degree oven for one hour or until garlic is tender.

Approximate values per tablespoon: 29 calories, 2 grams fat, no cholesterol, 4 grams carbohydrate, 223 milligrams sodium, 42 percent of calories from fat.

SEAFOOD CAKES WITH SALSA VERDE AND RED PEPPER AIOLI

Z'Tejas Grill

SCOTTSDALE, ARIZONA

Leo Madrigal, Chef

CRAB CAKES ARE ALWAYS FUN to serve to guests, but finding an equally exciting accompaniment for them can often be a challenge. These sensational seafood cakes are served with the chef's mouthwatering Salsa Verde and Red Pepper Aioli. You can make this dish as hot as you want by adding habañero chile peppers to the accompaniments.

> *5 pounds raw sole, cut into small pieces*
> *¾ cup mayonnaise*
> *2 tablespoons finely chopped ginger*
> *2 tablespoons finely chopped garlic*
> *1½ cups chopped green onion*
> *2 tablespoons Sambal chili paste*
> *2 cups fresh crabmeat*
> *4 cups Panko bread crumbs*
> *1 pound uncooked shrimp, shelled and chopped*
> *1 cup buttermilk*
> *2 eggs*
> *2 to 3 tablespoons canola oil*
> *Salsa Verde (recipe follows)*
> *Red Pepper Aioli (recipe follows)*

Place sole in a large bowl with the mayonnaise, ginger, garlic, green onion, chili paste, crabmeat, 2 cups of the bread crumbs, and shrimp. Mix well. Form into about 18 disks, each about 2½ inches across and ½ inch thick.

Beat buttermilk lightly with eggs in a small bowl. Place remaining 2 cups bread crumbs in a separate bowl. Dip both sides of each seafood cake into the egg wash, then into the bread crumbs, and set aside. (Cakes may be frozen at this point, then thawed in the refrigerator before cooking.)

In a large skillet, pan-fry seafood cakes in canola oil over medium-high heat for about 1 minute on each side, remove from pan, and sear on a flat grill for 3 minutes on each side. (Or you may finish cooking them on a cookie sheet in a 350-degree oven for 3 to 5 minutes.)

Spoon ¼ cup Salsa Verde on a round plate and place two cooked cakes on top of the sauce. Drizzle Red Pepper Aioli over cakes and salsa to serve.

MAKES 18 CAKES, ABOUT 9 APPETIZER SERVINGS

NOTE: *Sambal chili paste, a hot Asian sauce, and Panko bread crumbs can be found in specialty food stores and well-stocked grocery stores.*

SALSA VERDE

1 avocado, peeled and chopped

3 tomatillos, peeled and chopped

2 to 3 jalapeños, seeded

Salt and pepper to taste

2½ teaspoons lime juice

1½ teaspoons olive oil

¼ cup chopped fresh cilantro

1 cup water

Place all ingredients in a blender and purée until smooth. Warm over low heat until ready to serve.

MAKES ABOUT 1½ CUPS

CHICKEN SATAY WITH PEANUT SAUCE

Malee's on Main

SCOTTSDALE, ARIZONA

Deirdre Fawsett, Owner

CHICKEN SATAY WITH PEANUT SAUCE is great for those new to the flavors of Thai food. The sauce has a salty, sweet, and slightly sour taste.

2 pounds skinless, boneless chicken breasts, cut into 1-inch strips
3 cloves garlic, crushed
3 slices ginger, crushed
1 tablespoon curry powder
1 tablespoon ground coriander
1 teaspoon salt
Bamboo skewers soaked in water
1 cup coconut milk
Peanut Sauce (recipe follows)

Marinate the chicken in a mixture of the garlic, ginger, curry, coriander, and salt in the refrigerator for at least two hours.

Preheat an indoor or outdoor grill.

Thread a few pieces of chicken onto each bamboo stick and place on the grill. While cooking, sprinkle coconut milk over chicken. Grill until done. Serve with Peanut Sauce.

SERVES 8 TO 16

PEANUT SAUCE

1½ cups coconut milk
1 tablespoon Musman curry paste
1 tablespoon sugar
2 tablespoons peanut butter
1 tablespoon lemon juice
1 teaspoon salt

In a small saucepan, heat coconut milk over medium-high heat until boiling. Stir in the curry paste, sugar, peanut butter, lemon juice, and salt. Simmer until thickened, about 3 minutes.

MAKES ABOUT 1 CUP

NOTE: *Musman curry paste can be found at specialty stores and well-stocked grocery stores.*

Approximate values per serving (based on 8 servings): 350 calories, 25 grams fat, 73 milligrams cholesterol, 8 grams carbohydrate, 641 milligrams sodium, 62 percent of calories from fat.

BONELESS BUFFALO WINGS

Players Sports Bar

PHOENIX, ARIZONA

Robert Rosales, Executive Chef

THESE ADDICTIVE "WINGS" are served with a hot sauce that will send your temperature soaring. Serve with an ample supply of napkins and a fire extinguisher.

2¼ cups flour
1 tablespoon seasoned salt
¼ teaspoon ground cumin
¼ cup cornstarch
¼ teaspoon black pepper
1 tablespoon paprika
1½ teaspoons chili powder
1½ teaspoons salt
2½ pounds skinless, boneless chicken breasts, cut into strips
Canola oil for frying
Red Hot Sauce (recipe follows)

In a medium bowl, combine flour, seasoned salt, cumin, cornstarch, pepper, paprika, chili powder, and salt. Dredge chicken strips in flour mixture and deep fry in hot canola oil until golden brown. Drain on paper towels and serve with Red Hot Sauce.

MAKES 8 TO 12 APPETIZER SERVINGS

RED HOT SAUCE

1 cup of your favorite hot sauce
2 tablespoons butter, melted

Combine hot sauce and butter, stirring well.

MAKES ABOUT 1¼ CUPS

Approximate values per serving, including sauce: 485 calories, 32 grams fat, 76 milligrams cholesterol, 23 grams carbohydrate, 845 milligrams sodium, 60 percent of calories from fat.

CHICKEN LARB SALAD

Malee's on Main
SCOTTSDALE, ARIZONA

Deirdre Fawsett, Owner

LOOKING FOR AN INNOVATIVE APPETIZER? Try this unique dish of ground chicken meat, roasted ground rice, onions, and fresh mint wrapped in a cabbage leaf. You can also make it with ground beef or ground turkey. The flavors blend together exceptionally well; it will be hard to leave room for the main course.

1 tablespoon raw white rice
¾ pound ground chicken
½ tablespoon oyster sauce
½ tablespoon fish sauce
¾ teaspoon sugar
½ teaspoon paprika
10 fresh mint leaves
¼ cup julienned red onion

¼ cup chopped green onion

3 tablespoons lemon juice

1 head cabbage, quartered, leaves separated

Heat oven to 450 degrees. Roast rice on a sheet pan until light brown, about 3 minutes. Grind to a fine powder in a food processor or with a mortar and pestle. Set aside ¾ teaspoon of the powder.

In a large skillet over medium heat, lightly brown chicken, about 7 minutes. Add oyster sauce, fish sauce, sugar, roasted ground rice, paprika, mint leaves, red and green onions, and lemon juice. Mix well and cook 5 minutes more. Wrap in cabbage leaves and serve.

SERVES 4

Approximate values per serving: 260 calories, 9 grams fat, 80 milligrams cholesterol, 18 grams carbohydrate, 198 milligrams sodium, 29 percent of calories from fat

Soups

Pappa al Pomodoro

Franco's Trattoria

SCOTTSDALE, ARIZONA

Franco Fazzuoli, Chef/Owner, and Steve Martin, Partner

LOADS OF GARLIC, fresh tomatoes, and cubed Tuscan bread lend an enticing aroma and impressive flavor to this deliciously different soup.

1½ cups extra-virgin olive oil

6 cloves of garlic, mashed

1 large leek, chopped

1 small hot pepper, such as jalapeño or habañero, chopped

1½ pounds ripe, organic tomatoes, cored and chopped

10 large basil leaves, chopped

8 cups chicken or veal stock

1 loaf (approximately 1 pound, 2 ounces) hard-crust, day-old
*   Tuscan bread, cut into cubes*

Salt and pepper to taste

Heat 1 cup of the olive oil in a large saucepan over medium heat. Sauté the garlic, leek, and hot pepper until brown, about 5 minutes. Add the tomatoes and basil and simmer for 5 minutes more. Add the stock and bring to a boil. Gently stir in the cubed bread and season with salt and pepper. Let simmer for 5 more minutes.

Serve in bowls, each drizzled with a little more olive oil.

SERVES 8

NOTE: *Using day-old Tuscan bread in this recipe is a must, Chef Fazzuoli says. You can probably find it in most good bakeries. Another tip: Splurge on the olive oil—the higher the quality, the better the soup will taste.*

Approximate values per serving: 603 calories, 45 grams fat, no cholesterol, 40 grams carbohydrate, 1,160 milligrams sodium, 66 percent of calories from fat.

SOUP OF RED BELL PEPPERS

Christopher's Bistro

PHOENIX, ARIZONA

Christopher Gross, Chef, and Dawn Sullivan Ghee, Owner

THIS EXTREMELY RICH, extremely popular dish has been featured in *Bon Appetit* magazine. It is definitely worth splurging on.

4 tablespoons olive oil
7 medium red bell peppers, seeded and chopped
3 leeks, white part only, chopped
2 medium carrots, peeled and chopped
2 medium onions, chopped
7 cups rich chicken stock
2 potatoes, peeled and chopped
2 sprigs fresh thyme
1 bay leaf
6 cups heavy cream
8 tablespoons butter, sliced
Salt and freshly ground white pepper to taste

Heat 1 tablespoon olive oil in a large saucepan over medium-low heat. Sauté peppers, leeks, carrots, and onions until soft, about 10 minutes. Add stock, potatoes, thyme, and bay leaf. Increase heat and simmer until reduced by one-third, about 30 minutes.

Purée in a blender in batches. Strain soup back into the saucepan and add cream. Simmer 15 minutes or until reduced to desired consistency. Remove from heat and stir in remaining olive oil and butter until melted. Season with salt and white pepper to taste.

SERVES 6 TO 8

Approximate values per serving (based on 6 servings): 896 calories, 86 grams fat, 276 milligrams cholesterol, 26 grams carbohydrate, 1,020 milligrams sodium, 84 percent of calories from fat.

CREAM OF AVOCADO SOUP

Vincent Guerithault on Camelback

PHOENIX, ARIZONA

Vincent Guerithault, Chef/Owner

IT'S NO WONDER this chilled soup is a favorite—it is simply divine.

2 large avocados, peeled and diced
1 tablespoon chopped shallots
1 tablespoon olive oil
2 cups chicken stock, chilled
1 cup heavy whipping cream
Salt, pepper, and freshly grated nutmeg to taste
1 tomato, peeled, seeded, and diced

Purée avocados in blender until smooth. Sauté chopped shallots in olive oil for 2 to 3 minutes, but do not brown them. Set aside and let cool. In a large bowl, combine avocado purée with chilled chicken stock, whipping cream, and shallots. Whisk until smooth. Add salt, pepper, and nutmeg to taste. Serve chilled and topped with diced tomato.

SERVES 4

Approximate values per serving: 425 calories, 42 grams fat, 11 grams carbohydrate, 82 milligrams cholesterol, 423 milligrams sodium, 84 percent of calories from fat.

Caldo de Queso

The Grand Cafe

DOUGLAS, ARIZONA

Vanesa Vicente Quintana, Chef

DOUGLAS, ARIZONA, located in the far southeast corner of the state, may seem a little far to go for a good meal, but this delicious soup is worth the trip. A meal in itself, this soup is full of potatoes and green chiles and is topped with Monterey jack cheese.

1 tablespoon canola oil
1 pound potatoes, peeled and chopped
½ white onion, chopped
1 tomato, chopped
1 to 2 cloves garlic, chopped
8 cups water
1 cup green chiles, canned or fresh, cut into strips
Salt to taste
½ cup milk
2 to 3 tablespoons shredded Monterey jack cheese
Fried tortilla strips, for garnish (optional)

Heat oil over medium heat in a large stockpot. Add potatoes, onion, and tomato. Heat for 2 to 3 minutes. Add garlic and heat 6 to 8 minutes until onion is soft. Add water and bring to a boil. Boil until potatoes are soft, about 12 minutes. Reduce heat, then add green chiles, salt, and milk. To serve, top with cheese and tortilla strips.

SERVES 6 TO 8

Approximate values per serving: 100 calories, 4 grams fat, 5 milligrams cholesterol, 14 grams carbohydrate, 40 milligrams sodium, 34 percent of calories from fat.

MINESTRONE

Sandolo Restaurant at the Hyatt Regency Scottsdale at Gainey Ranch

SCOTTSDALE, ARIZONA

Anton Brunbauer, Executive Chef

FRESH BASIL AND OREGANO lend an extra special flavor to this soup. Serve it with hot Italian bread and lots of freshly grated Parmesan cheese.

1 gallon consommé or chicken stock

½ cup diced carrots

1 cup ditali pasta (or other small, cylindrical pasta), uncooked

1 cup diced celery

1 cup seeded, diced zucchini

1 cup seeded, diced tomatoes

1 cup diced yellow onion

1 cup green peas, fresh or frozen and thawed

2 tablespoons chopped fresh basil

2 tablespoons chopped fresh oregano

Salt and pepper to taste

3 to 4 tablespoons freshly grated Parmesan cheese

In a large stockpot, bring consommé to a boil over high heat. Add carrots, pasta, celery, zucchini, tomatoes, onion, peas, basil, and oregano. Reduce heat and simmer, uncovered, for 12 to 14 minutes, stirring occasionally. Season with salt and pepper. Garnish with Parmesan cheese.

SERVES 10

NOTE: *I cut this recipe in half when preparing it at home.*

Approximate values per serving: 114 calories, 1 gram fat, no cholesterol, 17 grams carbohydrate, 1,034 milligrams sodium, 3 percent of calories from fat.

COLD STRAWBERRY SOUP

Fuego Restaurant at the Doubletree Paradise Valley Resort

SCOTTSDALE, ARIZONA

Michael O'Dowd, Executive Chef

THIS ELEGANT SOUP can be prepared in minutes. Smooth and sweet, it is great for a champagne brunch.

16 ounces plain yogurt
16 ounces frozen strawberries with syrup, thawed
2 cups fresh strawberries, cored and quartered
2 tablespoons chopped fresh mint
12 ounces champagne

Combine yogurt, thawed and fresh strawberries, mint, and champagne in a blender or food processor. Purée until smooth. Refrigerate 30 minutes to 1 hour and serve chilled.

SERVES 6

Approximate values per serving: 169 calories, 3 grams fat, 10 milligrams cholesterol, 25 grams carbohydrate, 36 milligrams sodium, 18 percent of calories from fat.

ROYAL NORMAN'S CORN CILANTRO SOUP

The Biltmore Grill at the Arizona Biltmore

PHOENIX, ARIZONA

Bill Fox, Manager

THIS RECIPE comes from KTVK-Channel 3 weather forecaster Royal Norman and was used for a charity benefit by the Biltmore Grill. It is full of flavor and has just 5 grams of fat per serving.

2 teaspoons unsalted butter
1 teaspoon olive oil
1 medium onion, diced
2 garlic cloves, minced
1 teaspoon ground cumin
1 red bell pepper, chopped
1 green bell pepper, chopped
1 jalapeño, finely chopped
1 tomato, peeled, seeded, and chopped
2 cups corn kernels (fresh or frozen and thawed)
2 cups unsalted chicken stock
Salt to taste (optional)
3 tablespoons chopped cilantro

Melt butter and oil in a medium stockpot and sauté onion, garlic, and cumin until onion is translucent, about 3 minutes. Stir in bell peppers and jalapeño; cook until they start to soften, about 5 minutes more.

Add tomato, corn, and stock; reduce heat and simmer 20 minutes. Salt to taste, if desired.

Stir in cilantro just before serving.

SERVES 4

[26]

NOTE: *If this soup turns out too spicy for you, omit the jalapeño next time. Or, if you prefer it spicy, add a hotter variety of pepper.*

Approximate values per serving: 157 calories, 5 grams fat, 5 milligrams cholesterol, 26 grams carbohydrate, 536 milligrams sodium, 26 percent of calories from fat.

MUSHROOM BARLEY SOUP

Gooseberries

PHOENIX, ARIZONA

Ed Rengifo, Chef

THIS HEART-HEALTHY SOUP is sure to become a favorite in your household. It is full of vegetables and has a hint of lemon.

1 cup water
½ cup uncooked barley
4¾ cups chicken stock
1½ tablespoons butter
¾ cup diced onion
½ clove garlic, minced
6½ ounces button mushrooms, sliced (about 2¼ cups)
½ cup diced celery
¾ cup diced carrots
¼ teaspoon dried basil
1 lemon wedge
1 tablespoon fresh lemon juice
¼ teaspoon Tabasco sauce
¼ teaspoon Worcestershire sauce
⅛ teaspoon white pepper

In a small saucepan, bring water to a boil. Stir in barley, reduce heat, and cover. Simmer 8 to 10 minutes, or until tender. Remove from heat; let stand 5 minutes. Set aside.

Heat chicken stock over medium heat in a large stockpot. Melt butter in a medium sauté pan, add onion, garlic, mushrooms, celery, and carrots and sauté until tender, about 5 minutes. Add sautéed vegetables to chicken stock, stir in basil, lemon wedge, lemon juice, Tabasco sauce, Worcestershire sauce, white pepper, and cooked barley.

Simmer, uncovered, for 20 minutes; remove lemon wedge and serve.

SERVES 8

Approximate values per serving: 90 calories, 3 grams fat, 6 milligrams cholesterol, 10 grams carbohydrates, 564 milligrams sodium, 30 percent of calories from fat.

GRILLED CORN SOUP WITH ANCHO CHILE CREAM

Vincent Guerithault on Camelback

PHOENIX, ARIZONA

Vincent Guerithault, Chef/Owner

WHEN THE DAY IS CHILLY, Southwest Corn Chowder may be just what is called for. This hearty soup is outstanding.

> *4 ears corn*
> *2 cloves garlic, peeled*
> *½ cup diced carrots*
> *½ cup diced onion*
> *¼ cup diced celery*
> *1 jalapeño, finely diced*
> *1½ cups chicken stock*

1 cup half-and-half
Ancho Chile Cream (recipe follows)

Preheat a grill.

Shuck corn and remove silk. Grill ears of corn for 5 minutes over a hot flame. Cut corn from ears. Combine cut corn with garlic, carrots, onion, celery, jalapeño, and chicken stock in a large saucepan and simmer for 30 minutes. Add half-and-half and boil for 5 minutes.

Place in a blender and purée until smooth. Serve hot, with 1 tablespoon of blended Ancho Chile Cream swirled in each serving of soup.

SERVES 4 TO 6

Approximate values per serving (based on 4 servings): 761 calories, 18 grams fat, 28 milligrams cholesterol, 136 grams carbohydrate, 475 milligrams sodium, 20 percent of calories from fat.

ANCHO CHILE CREAM

1 ancho chile (or ¼ cup paprika)
3 tablespoons half-and-half
1 tablespoon sour cream

Place ancho chile (or paprika) and half-and-half in a small saucepan and simmer for 5 minutes. Remove from heat, cool, and stir in sour cream.

MAKES 4 TABLESPOONS

GAZPACHO

Sprouts Restaurant at Marriott's Camelback Inn Resort

SCOTTSDALE, ARIZONA

Gary Scherer, Executive Chef

YOU MAY ALREADY HAVE a gazpacho recipe, but you just might abandon it for this version accompanied by crostini.

> 2 medium tomatoes, chopped
> 2½ cucumbers, peeled, seeded, and chopped
> ½ white onion, chopped
> 1 red bell pepper, seeded and chopped
> ¼ cup red pimientos
> 2 cloves garlic, chopped
> 1 cup V-8 juice
> 2 teaspoons Tabasco sauce
> Salt and pepper to taste
> Roasted corn, cooked black beans, and fresh cilantro for garnish
> Crostini (recipe follows)

Combine the tomatoes, cucumbers, onion, bell pepper, pimientos, garlic, V-8 juice, and Tabasco in a food processor. Purée until smooth.

Season with salt and pepper. If desired, garnish with roasted corn kernels (spread corn kernels on a baking sheet; roast in a 400-degree oven for 3 to 5 minutes until kernels start to brown), black beans, and fresh cilantro. Serve with crostini.

SERVES 4

Approximate values per serving of soup: 94 calories, 1 gram fat, no cholesterol, 21 grams carbohydrate, 250 milligrams sodium, 6 percent of calories from fat.

CROSTINI

¼ cup whole garlic cloves, peeled (about 6)
¾ cup olive oil
Focaccia bread

Combine garlic cloves and olive oil in a small saucepan. Simmer for 10 minutes over medium heat and strain, reserving the oil. Lightly brush the focaccia with the strained oil. Grill lightly or heat in a 350-degree oven for 5 to 10 minutes.

SERVES 8

Approximate values per serving of crostini: 200 calories, 21 grams fat, no cholesterol, 4 grams carbohydrate, 21 milligrams sodium, 90 percent of calories from fat.

SWEET AND SPICY CHILI

Sprouts Restaurant at Marriott's Camelback Inn Resort
SCOTTSDALE, ARIZONA

Gary Scherer, Executive Chef

THE SECRET OF THIS SOUP is in the chili sauce, which is well worth the extra time it takes for the preparation.

1½ cups pinto beans, canned or dried
1 pound chuck roast, 1-inch dice
½ cup diced yellow onion
⅔ cup diced green bell pepper
1 teaspoon minced garlic
¼ cup chili powder

1 teaspoon ground cumin
½ teaspoon cayenne
1½ cups fresh, diced tomatoes
1½ cups Chili Sauce (recipe follows)
1½ cups beef stock
Salt and pepper to taste

If using dried beans, soak them overnight in 4½ cups cold water. Drain and rinse.

Sauté beef in a medium skillet over medium heat until evenly browned. Drain off excess fat. Add onion, green pepper, and garlic and sauté lightly. Blend in chili powder, cumin, and cayenne. Let simmer for a few minutes, stirring constantly.

Blend in tomatoes, Chili Sauce, pinto beans, and beef stock. Let simmer for 30 minutes to 1 hour or until slightly thickened, stirring occasionally. Season with salt and pepper to taste.

SERVES 12

CHILI SAUCE

2 medium red chile peppers
2 tablespoons diced onion
1 teaspoon olive oil
1 teaspoon tequila
1 cup chicken stock
Salt and pepper to taste

Sauté chile peppers and onion in olive oil in a small pan. Add tequila and chicken stock and simmer for 5 minutes. Place in a blender and blend to a smooth consistency. Season with salt and pepper.

MAKES 1½ CUPS

Approximate values per serving: 203 calories, 8 grams fat, 26 milligrams cholesterol, 20 grams carbohydrate, 240 milligrams sodium, 36 percent of calories from fat.

CREAM OF ADOBO CHICKEN SOUP

Ventanas at the Scottsdale Princess Resort

SCOTTSDALE, ARIZONA

Reed Groban, Executive Chef

THIS PERFECTLY SEASONED SOUP is rich, smooth, and wonderful.

2 quarts chicken stock
2½ tablespoons flour
1½ tablespoons melted butter
¼ cup Adobo Marinade, plus extra to taste (recipe follows)
3 tablespoons heavy cream
One 4-ounce skinless, boneless chicken breast half, cooked and diced
Diced tomatoes, fresh cilantro, and cornbread croutons for garnish

Bring chicken stock to a boil in a large stockpot. Meanwhile, combine flour and melted butter to form a roux. Add enough of the roux to stock to thicken to a cream-soup consistency. Add Adobo Marinade and allow to cook for 30 minutes. Add additional marinade to taste.

Blend in heavy cream and allow to cook for an additional 15 minutes. Adjust consistency with more roux if desired, allowing enough time for the mixture to thicken slightly. Add diced chicken; let heat through.

Garnish with tomatoes, cilantro, and cornbread croutons.

SERVES 8

ADOBO MARINADE

2½ ounces ancho chiles

1 whole bulb garlic, roasted (for roasting instructions, see page 9)

2 teaspoons chipotle peppers in adobo sauce

¼ cup chopped cilantro

¼ cup chopped red onion

1½ tablespoons chili powder

2¼ teaspoons ground cumin

2 teaspoons cinnamon

¾ teaspoon cayenne pepper

2¼ teaspoons dried oregano

1¼ teaspoons ground black pepper

1¼ teaspoons kosher salt

¼ cup lemon juice

¼ cup cider vinegar

¼ cup soy sauce

½ cup sesame oil

Remove seeds from the ancho chiles and discard. Soak chiles in warm water for 20 minutes.

Combine all ingredients except sesame oil in a food processor and purée to a fine paste. Add oil in a slow stream until well incorporated and emulsified.

MAKES 1 CUP

NOTE: *Ancho chiles and chipotle peppers can be found in specialty grocery stores. Chipotle peppers are frequently sold prepared in jars.*

Approximate values per serving: 180 calories, 11 grams fat, 41 milligrams cholesterol, 4 grams carbohydrate, 921 milligrams sodium, 58 percent of calories from fat.

SALADS

By request

By Betsy Mann
Special for food

WARM YUKON GOLD POTATO SALAD

Eddie's Grill

PHOENIX, ARIZONA

Eddie Matney, Chef

WHEN I FIRST PREPARED THIS POTATO SALAD, everyone asked the secret of its delicious taste. I have yet to find another potato salad with such a distinctive flavor. At the restaurant, Chef Matney serves a medium-rare beef fillet over the warm salad and tops it off with Vidalia Onion Rings (see page 57).

1½ pounds Yukon gold potatoes (about 2 medium, quartered)
2 tablespoons olive oil
6 cloves garlic, chopped
1 shallot, chopped
¼ pound prosciutto, julienned
½ pound portabello mushrooms, sliced
8 ounces fresh spinach
1 tablespoon chopped fresh rosemary
Balsamic vinegar to taste
Dash of Worcestershire sauce
Salt and pepper to taste

In a large pan of water, boil unpeeled potatoes until soft, about 15 minutes. Drain. Heat olive oil in a large sauté pan over medium heat. Sauté potatoes, garlic, shallot, prosciutto, and mushrooms for 5 minutes, or until mushrooms are soft. Add spinach, rosemary, vinegar, Worcestershire sauce, and salt and pepper. Sauté until spinach wilts, about 3 to 5 minutes. Serve warm.

SERVES 4

Approximate values per serving: 294 calories, 10 grams fat, 20 milligrams cholesterol, 39 grams carbohydrate, 826 milligrams sodium, 29 percent of calories from fat.

Bleu Cheese Vinaigrette

The Teacup Dining Room at the Hassayampa Inn
PRESCOTT, ARIZONA

Randall Bonneville, Executive Chef

THIS POPULAR HOUSE DRESSING boasts the flavors of sautéed garlic, bleu cheese, and a hint of Tabasco to add a delightful taste to any salad.

2½ tablespoons minced garlic
½ cup plus 2 tablespoons olive oil
1 pinch dried oregano
½ teaspoon dried basil
½ cup salad oil
1 tablespoon black pepper
2 teaspoons salt
1½ tablespoons freshly squeezed lemon juice
½ cup sugar
2 tablespoons white vinegar
3 tablespoons water
2 teaspoons Tabasco sauce
4 ounces bleu cheese, crumbled

In a small saucepan over medium heat, sauté garlic in 2 tablespoons of the olive oil for about 2 minutes. Add oregano and basil. In a medium bowl, combine ½ cup olive oil, salad oil, black pepper, salt, lemon juice, sugar, vinegar, water, Tabasco, and bleu cheese. Add the sautéed garlic and blend with a wire whip. Refrigerate before serving.

MAKES APPROXIMATELY 2 CUPS

Approximate values per 2 tablespoons: 188 calories, 17 grams fat, 5 milligrams cholesterol, 7 grams carbohydrate, 366 milligrams sodium, 81 percent of calories from fat.

SALAD OF ASPARAGUS AND MILD ROASTED PEPPERS WITH HONEY AND SHERRY WINE VINEGAR DRESSING

Vincent Guerithault on Camelback

PHOENIX, ARIZONA

Vincent Guerithault, Chef/Owner

THIS HEART-SMART fresh asparagus salad is too good to miss.

20 stalks asparagus, peeled
1 yellow bell pepper
1 red bell pepper
Honey and Sherry Wine Vinegar Dressing (recipe follows)
2 tablespoons chopped fresh basil
2 tablespoons peeled, diced tomato

Blanch asparagus; let cool. Roast bell peppers over a hot grill until skin blackens and begins to bubble. Peel, removing any seeds. Cut into julienne strips. On a large plate, weave yellow and red bell peppers. Place asparagus across top. Drizzle with dressing and top with basil and tomato.

SERVES 4

HONEY AND SHERRY WINE VINEGAR DRESSING

2 tablespoons honey
2 teaspoons sherry wine vinegar
Salt and pepper to taste

In a small bowl, blend all ingredients, mixing well.

MAKES ¼ CUP

Approximate values per serving: 69 calories, no fat, no cholesterol, 16 grams carbohydrate, 305 milligrams sodium.

APPLE JICAMA SLAW WITH HONEY CHIPOTLE VINAIGRETTE

Sam's Cafe

PHOENIX AND SCOTTSDALE, ARIZONA

Tudie Frank Johnson, Corporate Chef

TART, CRUNCHY, AND REFRESHING, this excellent salad makes a wonderful, snappy accompaniment to any summertime meal.

½ pound jicama, peeled and sliced into ¼-inch-thick julienne
2 Granny Smith apples, cored and sliced into ¼-inch-thick julienne
1 medium red bell pepper, seeds and stem removed,
  sliced into ¼-inch-thick julienne
Honey Chipotle Vinaigrette (recipe follows)
Salt and pepper to taste
Chopped cilantro to taste

Combine all ingredients in a large container. Cover and chill.

SERVES 4

HONEY CHIPOTLE VINAIGRETTE

¼ cup water
¼ cup red wine vinegar
¼ cup Dijon mustard
¼ teaspoon dried basil
¼ teaspoon dried oregano
¼ teaspoon dried dill
¼ teaspoon dried thyme
¼ teaspoon sugar
1 small clove garlic, minced
1 teaspoon black pepper

¼ tablespoon salt
2 cups salad oil
¼ cup honey
1 chipotle chile in adobo

Mix water, vinegar, mustard, basil, oregano, dill, thyme, sugar, garlic, black pepper, and salt in blender or food processor. Slowly whisk in oil until thickened. In a separate blender container, purée honey and chipotle chile together; whisk into vinaigrette.

MAKES APPROXIMATELY 2½ CUPS

NOTE: *Chipotle peppers in adobo sauce are frequently found in the Southwestern or Mexican ingredients sections of markets.*

Approximate values per serving: 142 calories, 9 grams fat, 16 grams carbohydrate, no cholesterol, 84 milligrams sodium, 54 percent of calories from fat.

GRILLED CHICKEN WITH MACADAMIA NUTS

The Terrace Dining Room at the Wigwam Resort

LITCHFIELD PARK, ARIZONA

Arthur Acedo, Chef

THIS EXTRAORDINARY SALAD is served at the resort's brunches with a spicy Ginger Chili Vinaigrette that sets it apart from the rest.

1 pound skinless, boneless chicken breasts, cut into bite-size pieces
¼ cup chopped green onion
1 cup roughly chopped honey-roasted macadamia nuts
½ cup fresh orange sections
2 tablespoons finely diced or julienned red bell pepper
Ginger Chili Vinaigrette (recipe follows)

Grill chicken, or bake in a 350-degree oven for 20 minutes, until chicken is no longer pink. Cool. In a medium salad bowl, combine cooled chicken, green onion, nuts, orange sections, and bell pepper. Serve with Ginger Chili Vinaigrette.

SERVES 4 TO 6

GINGER CHILI VINAIGRETTE

½ teaspoon fresh, minced ginger
¾ teaspoon chopped chipotle pepper
¼ teaspoon chopped onion
¼ teaspoon chopped garlic
1½ teaspoons chopped pimientos
Pinch of salt
Pinch of black pepper
1 tablespoon chopped fresh parsley
1 tablespoon pasteurized egg substitute
¼ cup tarragon vinegar
¼ cup fresh orange juice
½ cup corn oil

In a blender, combine ginger, chipotle pepper, onion, garlic, pimientos, salt, pepper, parsley, egg substitute, vinegar, and orange juice. Blend well. Slowly add oil, blending until well combined. Chill before serving.

MAKES ABOUT 1 CUP

Approximate values per serving (salad with 2 tablespoons of Ginger Chili Vinaigrette): 329 calories, 22 grams fat, 66 milligrams cholesterol, 6 grams carbohydrate, 27 grams protein, 98 milligrams sodium, 60 percent of calories from fat.

CHOPPED CABBAGE SALAD

Havana Café

SCOTTSDALE AND PHOENIX, ARIZONA

B. J. Henderson, Chef/Owner

DON'T COUNT ON THIS salad staying around very long when you make it. Lime juice and fresh cilantro make it tangy and unfailingly good. This salad is best when served the same day it is made and is not too cold.

8 cups coarsely chopped green cabbage
½ teaspoon salt
½ teaspoon garlic powder
½ teaspoon sugar
¼ teaspoon white pepper
2 tablespoons lime juice
2 tablespoons olive oil
¼ cup fresh chopped cilantro

In a large bowl, combine all ingredients. Toss well and refrigerate for two hours or longer to enhance flavors.

SERVES 8

Approximate values per serving: 51 calories, 4 grams fat, no cholesterol, 5 grams carbohydrate, 147 milligrams sodium, 58 percent of calories from fat.

RASPBERRY-CRANBERRY GELATIN SALAD

Aunt Pittypat's Pantry

GLENDALE, ARIZONA

Mel Foehner and Sue Branch, Owners

THIS PRETTY SALAD makes a special holiday luncheon dish.

1 can (20 ounces) crushed pineapple
1 box (6 ounces) raspberry gelatin
8 ounces cream cheese, softened
2 tablespoons mayonnaise
1 can (16 ounces) whole-berry cranberry sauce
2 cups chopped walnuts
2 cups Cool Whip

Drain pineapple, reserving juice in a measuring cup, and add water to juice to measure 1 cup.

In a saucepan, heat juice to boiling, remove from stove, and stir in raspberry gelatin. When gelatin is dissolved, pour into a medium bowl with softened cream cheese and mayonnaise. Mix until cheese is well incorporated. Add pineapple, cranberry sauce, and walnuts, stirring well. Fold in Cool Whip and turn into a 9 x 13-inch baking pan. Chill in refrigerator until set, about 2 hours.

SERVES 12

Approximate values per serving: 388 calories, 24 grams fat, 22 milligrams cholesterol, 120 milligrams sodium, 41 grams carbohydrate, 52 percent of calories from fat.

Curry Chicken Salad

Country Glazed Ham Company

SCOTTSDALE, ARIZONA

Mike Hill, Owner

THIS DO-AHEAD SALAD is good to serve as a luncheon dish.

2 pounds skinless, boneless chicken breasts, poached and cubed
¼ cup black currants
½ cup mayonnaise
¼ cup sour cream
¼ bunch celery, diced small
Curry Sauce (recipe follows)

In a large bowl, combine chicken, currants, mayonnaise, sour cream, and celery. Stir in Curry Sauce and mix well. Refrigerate for at least 3 hours before serving.

SERVES 4.

CURRY SAUCE

3 tablespoons Sharwood's Bengal Hot Chutney, or any
*   mango chutney*
2 tablespoons fresh lemon juice
¼ cup curry powder
1 cup sour cream

Process all ingredients in a food processor until well blended.

MAKES APPROXIMATELY 1½ CUPS

Approximate values per serving: 791 calories, 59 grams fat, 193 milligrams cholesterol, 15 grams carbohydrate, 377 milligrams sodium, 67 percent of calories from fat.

SOUTHWEST CAESAR DRESSING

Hyatt Regency Scottsdale at Gainey Ranch
SCOTTSDALE, ARIZONA

Anton Brunbauer, Executive Chef

I FIRST TASTED THIS DRESSING at a wonderful banquet at the Hyatt Regency. It surely is a perfection of flavors and will earn your highest accolades.

1 cup mayonnaise
1 teaspoon brown sugar
2 tablespoons soy sauce
3 tablespoons lemon juice
½ teaspoon cayenne
2 tablespoons grated Parmesan cheese
Salt and pepper to taste

In a small bowl, combine mayonnaise, brown sugar, soy sauce, lemon juice, cayenne, and Parmesan cheese; blend well. Add salt and pepper to taste. Serve over mixed greens or your favorite salad.

MAKES APPROXIMATELY 1 CUP, SERVES 4 TO 5

Approximate values per 2 tablespoons: 208 calories, 2 grams fat, 17 milligrams cholesterol, 2 grams carbohydrate, 380 milligrams sodium, 94 percent of calories from fat.

SONORAN COLE SLAW

The Good Egg

PHOENIX, ARIZONA

Matt Trussela, Director of Operations

THIS EXCELLENT SALAD makes a beautiful presentation and the tangy dressing gives it quite a kick.

½ head green cabbage, shredded
½ cup shredded red cabbage
2 tablespoons shredded carrots
½ cup diced celery
½ cup diced onion
¼ cup diced green bell pepper
¼ cup diced red bell pepper
Dressing (recipe follows)

In a large bowl, combine shredded cabbages and carrots, celery, onion, and bell peppers. Pour dressing over mixture; stir well to combine. Refrigerate until ready to serve.

SERVES 10, ½ CUP EACH

DRESSING

2 tablespoons mayonnaise
2 tablespoons honey
2 tablespoons seasoned rice vinegar
2 tablespoons red wine vinegar
1½ teaspoons salad oil
1 tablespoon sugar
1½ teaspoons dry mustard
¾ teaspoon black pepper

½ teaspoon salt
1 dash granulated garlic
1 tablespoon finely chopped fresh cilantro

Combine all ingredients, stirring well.

Approximate values per serving: 52 calories, 3 grams fat, 2 milligrams cholesterol, 7 grams carbohydrate, 133 milligrams sodium, 48 percent of calories from fat.

SPINACH-RICE SALAD

Cork 'N Cleaver

PHOENIX, ARIZONA

Tommy Growney, Co-owner

SPINACH-RICE SALAD is a simple dish, but wonderfully flavorful. It makes a memorable salad or side dish.

2 cups white rice, cooked and refrigerated to cool
½ cup herb vinaigrette dressing (your choice)
1 tablespoon soy sauce
½ teaspoon sugar
¾ cup julienned spinach
½ cup diced celery
½ cup diced green onion
2 slices bacon, cooked and crumbled

Transfer cooled rice to a medium bowl and add vinaigrette, soy sauce, and sugar; mix well. Add spinach, celery, and green onion; toss all together. Sprinkle with crumbled bacon before serving.

SERVES 4

Approximate values per serving: 300 calories, 16 grams fat, 10 milligrams cholesterol, 35 grams carbohydrate, 340 milligrams sodium, 40 percent of calories from fat.

ORCHID NOODLE SALAD

The Vintage Market

PHOENIX, ARIZONA

Vitaly Feygin, Owner

THIS DELICIOUS MEDLEY OF SHRIMP, stir-fried pork, soba noodles, and snow peas can easily serve as a luncheon dish all on its own. It's become one of my favorites.

1 pound soba noodles (or spaghetti), cooked al dente
1 cup julienned red bell pepper
2 to 3 green onions, finely chopped
½ cup julienned snow peas
1 cup water chestnuts, drained
1½ cups bay shrimp, fully cooked
½ pound stir-fried pork or chicken, thinly julienned
Dressing (recipe follows)

In a large bowl, combine all ingredients. Add dressing and toss well. Refrigerate or allow to sit for 30 minutes before serving.

SERVES 8 TO 10 AS A SIDE DISH

NOTE: *Ingredients in this recipe that are not available at your grocery store can be found at Asian grocery markets.*

DRESSING

3 tablespoons toasted sesame oil
1 tablespoon mushroom soy sauce
1 tablespoon garlic chili paste (this is very hot!), or to taste

Place all ingredients in a small bowl and combine thoroughly.

Approximate values per serving: 347 calories, 7 grams total fat, 83 milligrams cholesterol, 50 grams carbohydrate, 941 milligrams sodium, 17 percent of calories from fat.

SIDE DISHES

Green Chile Mashed Potatoes

Sam's Cafe

PHOENIX AND SCOTTSDALE, ARIZONA

Tudie Frank Johnson, Corporate Chef

SAM'S CAFE ADDS a Southwestern kick to mashed potatoes with roasted poblano peppers.

2 poblano peppers, roasted, peeled, and diced
2½ pounds new red potatoes, unpeeled (about 5 or 6)
½ cup diced carrots
8 tablespoons butter
½ cup sour cream
3 tablespoons chopped green onion
Salt and pepper to taste

To roast poblanos, grill entire pepper over a hot flame (or rotate under a broiler) until skin chars. Place in a paper bag, close, and set aside. In about 10 minutes, skin will loosen and you can peel it off easily. Remove seeds.

Dice roasted poblanos into small pieces. Cut potatoes into quarters and boil in a large pot of water until soft, about 12 to 15 minutes. In microwave or another saucepan, cook carrots with a small amount of water until softened but still crisp, then drain.

Drain and mash potatoes with butter and sour cream. Add carrots, green onion, and poblanos; mix well. Season with salt and pepper.

SERVES 4 TO 6

Approximate values per serving: 409 calories, 23 grams fat, 59 milligrams cholesterol, 46 grams carbohydrate, 432 milligrams sodium, 50 percent of calories from fat.

Sweet Corn Tomalito

Chevy's Mexican Restaurant

PHOENIX, ARIZONA

THIS SCRUMPTIOUS DISH is like a cornbread stuffing—and easy to prepare. It should have a smooth, moist texture.

5 tablespoons margarine, softened

¼ cup masa

⅓ cup sugar

2 cups corn kernels, fresh or frozen and thawed

½ cup water

½ cup cornmeal

1 teaspoon baking powder

½ teaspoon salt

2 tablespoons plus 1 teaspoon milk

In a small bowl, mix the margarine, masa, and sugar using an electric mixer until light and fluffy, about 1 minute.

Blend half the corn kernels with the water in a blender until smooth. Combine this mixture with the margarine mixture, stirring well. Add the remaining corn kernels, cornmeal, baking powder, salt, and milk, and mix well.

Bring a medium saucepan of water to a boil. Pour the corn mixture into an 8-inch-square baking dish. Tightly cover with plastic wrap and set atop the saucepan of boiling water. Keep pan tightly wrapped and steam for 50 minutes to 1 hour (check water level often), until a toothpick inserted in the center comes out clean.

SERVES 12 TO 16

NOTE: *Masa, a Mexican corn flour, can be found in well-stocked supermarkets and ethnic food stores.*

Approximate values per serving: 87 calories, 4 grams fat, no cholesterol, 13 grams carbohydrate, 119 milligrams sodium, 36 percent of calories from fat.

GARLIC MASHED POTATOES

Sfuzzi

SCOTTSDALE AND GLENDALE, ARIZONA

ONE OF THE MOST REQUESTED RECIPES is for mashed pota-
toes. The three recipes in this collection are all outstanding variations
of this irresistible comfort food. "Heaven on earth" is how Sfuzzi's version could be described. The wonderful aroma and flavor of roasted
garlic make them irresistible.

> *6 cloves roasted garlic, chopped (for roasting instructions, see page 9)*
> *Olive oil*
> *1 pound new potatoes, unpeeled (3 or 4)*
> *¾ cup heavy whipping cream*
> *2 tablespoons butter*
> *Salt and pepper to taste*
> *Freshly chopped parsley for garnish*

Cut potatoes into quarters. In a large pot, bring potatoes to a
boil over medium-high heat. Boil until soft, about 12 to 15 minutes.
Mash, then add whipping cream and the chopped, roasted garlic.
Add butter, then salt and pepper to taste. Top with a dash of chopped
parsley.

SERVES 2 GENEROUSLY

Approximate values per serving: 500 calories, 27 grams fat, 79 milligrams cholesterol,
56 grams carbohydrate, 313 milligrams sodium, 48 percent of calories from fat.

SCALLOPED POTATOES

Bola's Grill at the Holiday Inn Old Town Scottsdale

SCOTTSDALE, ARIZONA

Craig Nassar, Executive Chef

THIS INCREDIBLY RICH DISH, served at Bola's Grill for Sunday brunch, is a great accompaniment to any meal.

1½ pounds Idaho russet potatoes
1 quart heavy cream
1 tablespoon chicken broth
2 tablespoons chopped fresh oregano
2 tablespoons chopped fresh thyme
¼ pound Parmesan cheese, grated (about 1½ cups)
Salt and pepper to taste

Grease an 8 x 12-inch casserole dish.

Wash and peel potatoes; cut into ½-inch slices, and set aside.

In a large saucepan, combine cream, chicken broth, oregano, and thyme and bring to a boil. Reduce heat to a simmer. Stir in 1 cup of the Parmesan cheese and continue to simmer for 15 minutes. Add salt and pepper to taste.

Preheat oven to 350 degrees.

Cover bottom of pan with a layer of sauce, then one layer of potatoes. Continue until potato mixture is about half an inch from top of pan. End with a layer of sauce and remaining ½ cup of Parmesan cheese.

Cover with foil and bake for 35 to 45 minutes, until potatoes pierce easily with a fork. Remove foil for last 10 minutes to brown the top. Let stand for 15 minutes before serving.

SERVES 8

Approximate values per serving: 550 calories, 46 grams fat, 175 milligrams cholesterol, 20 grams carbohydrate, 177 milligrams sodium, 75 percent of calories from fat.

STUFFED ROMAINE LETTUCE

The Coyote Grill

PHOENIX, ARIZONA

Chris Harter, Owner

THIS DELICIOUS SIDE DISH consists of mushrooms, onions, Parmesan cheese, and bacon rolled inside romaine lettuce.

1 head romaine lettuce
Salt and pepper to taste
1 pound bacon, diced
1 clove garlic, minced
2 large yellow onions, chopped
2 cups sliced mushrooms
¼ cup chicken stock
1 teaspoon cornstarch
¼ cup shredded Parmesan cheese
Diced pimientos for garnish

Preheat oven to 350 degrees.

Bring a large pot of lightly salted water to a boil. Add uncut head of washed romaine and boil for about 1 minute. Drain water and cover lettuce immediately with ice water to keep the color green. Drain lettuce after cooling and lay it on a cutting board. Remove the core and open the lettuce flat to expose the heart. Cover lettuce with plastic wrap and flatten with a meat-tenderizing hammer or the bottom of a sauté pan. Remove plastic wrap and season lettuce with salt and pepper.

In a separate pan, sauté bacon until slightly brown. Add garlic, onions, and mushrooms. Cook until onions are soft, about 3 minutes. Cool mixture.

Preheat oven to 350 degrees.

[54]

Place onion-bacon mixture on half of the flattened lettuce. Fold the other half over tightly and place on a baking sheet.

Bake for 10 minutes, until hot all the way through.

Add cornstarch to chicken stock. Remove stuffed lettuce from oven and cut into ten 2½-inch slices. Glaze with thickened chicken stock and top with Parmesan cheese. Garnish with pimientos.

SERVES 10

Approximate values per serving: 290 calories, 23 grams fat, 40 milligrams cholesterol, 4 grams carbohydrate, 817 milligrams sodium, 73 percent of calories from fat.

DIRTY RICE

Baby Kay's

SCOTTSDALE AND PHOENIX, ARIZONA

Baby Kay Romero, Owner

THIS CLASSIC CAJUN DISH is great as a side dish to, say, crawfish etouffée, or as a main course.

¼ pound hot pork sausage
1 pound ground beef
Cayenne to taste
Black pepper to taste
Salt to taste
1 onion, chopped
2 stalks celery, chopped
½ green bell pepper, chopped
1½ cups cooked long-grain white rice

In a large skillet, brown the sausage and ground beef over medium heat. Add cayenne, black pepper, and salt to taste. Add onion, celery, and bell pepper, and cook until tender, about 5 minutes. Stir in cooked rice and serve.

SERVES 4 AS A MAIN DISH, 6 TO 8 AS A SIDE DISH

Approximate values per serving as a main dish: 386 calories, 28 grams fat, 77 milligrams cholesterol, 16 grams carbohydrate, 190 milligrams sodium, 66 percent of calories from fat.

P. B. C. Mashers

Prescott Brewing Company

PRESCOTT, ARIZONA

Karl Klein, Executive Chef

GARLIC AND SOUR CREAM help make these mashed potatoes from the Prescott Brewing Company irresistibly delicious. This version is especially popular with kids.

4½ pounds red potatoes
8 tablespoons butter
¾ teaspoon black pepper
1½ teaspoons salt
⅛ cup sour cream
⅛ cup half-and-half
1½ teaspoons granulated garlic

Wash and scrub potatoes (do not peel). Boil potatoes in a large pot of water until soft, about 20 minutes. Drain water and add butter, pepper, salt, sour cream, half-and-half, and granulated garlic. Mash until creamy and serve immediately.

SERVES 8

Approximate values per serving: 328 calories, 14 grams fat, 37 milligrams cholesterol, 46 grams carbohydrate, 545 milligrams sodium, 38 percent of calories from fat.

VIDALIA ONION RINGS

Eddie's Grill

PHOENIX, ARIZONA

Eddie Matney, Chef

MAKE A BIG BATCH of these onion rings and watch as they disappear—quickly. Chef Matney serves these scrumptious onion rings on top of a medium-rare fillet and his Warm Yukon Gold Potato Salad (see recipe on page 36).

> *1 Vidalia onion*
> *2 cups flour*
> *1 teaspoon dried thyme*
> *1 pinch dried marjoram*
> *1 pinch granulated garlic*
> *1 cup buttermilk*
> *2 cups vegetable oil*

Slice onion into 1-inch slices and separate into rings, to make about 16 onion rings. In a medium bowl combine flour, thyme, marjoram, and garlic. Pour buttermilk in a separate bowl. Heat oil for deep frying. Dip onion rings in buttermilk, then in seasoned flour. Deep-fry until golden brown.

SERVES 4

Approximate values per serving: 375 calories, 28 grams fat, 1 milligram cholesterol, 27 grams carbohydrate, 170 milligrams sodium, 67 percent of calories from fat.

TEXAS CAVIAR

NM Cafe at Neiman Marcus

SCOTTSDALE, ARIZONA

Anthony Bespa, General Manager

PREPARED IN MINUTES, this delightfully different side dish consists of a mouth-watering blend of black-eyed peas and Jamaican relish.

1 can (16 ounces) black-eyed peas
⅓ cup Jamaican relish
2½ tablespoons cider vinegar
½ cup chopped onion
2 cloves garlic, chopped
Dash of salt
Dash of white pepper

Place all ingredients in a mixing bowl and stir by hand or with a wooden spoon. Refrigerate for one or two hours to allow flavors to blend. Serve as a side dish with salads or sandwiches.

MAKES 4 SERVINGS, ½ CUP EACH

NOTE: *Jamaican relish can be found at Neiman Marcus or specialty food stores.*

Approximate values per serving: 210 calories, 1 gram fat, no cholesterol, 40 grams carbohydrate, 96 milligrams sodium, 3 percent of calories from fat.

MAIN COURSES

BEFF

WINEBURGERS

Harvey's Wineburgers
PHOENIX, ARIZONA

Tom D'Angelo, Cook/Bartender

THE INGREDIENTS OF THIS BURGER are nothing out of the ordinary, but after your first bite, trust me: You'll never want a regular hamburger again.

> *1½ pounds lean ground beef*
> *Seasoning salt to taste*
> *2½ cups Burgundy wine*
> *4 slices American or Swiss cheese*
> *4 hamburger buns*

Heat a grill.

Form ground beef into four 5- to 6-ounce patties. Place patties onto grill and season lightly with seasoning salt. Cook for about 3 minutes, then flip patties over. Cook 1 or 2 minutes longer, then pour 6 to 8 ounces (about ¾ to 1 cup) of wine slowly onto each patty to drench.

Cook until medium or medium well. Top with cheese and serve on buns.

SERVES 4

Approximate values per serving: 784 calories, 46 grams fat, 154 milligrams cholesterol, 25 grams carbohydrate, 550 milligrams sodium, 62 percent of calories from fat.

BEEF PANANG

Malee's on Main

SCOTTSDALE, ARIZONA

Deirdre Fawsett, Owner

COCONUT MILK lends unique flavor to this Thai dish.

1 tablespoon canola oil
2 tablespoons Panang curry paste
1 cup sliced beef tenderloin
1 cup sliced green bell pepper
½ cup sliced carrots
1 tablespoon fish sauce
1 tablespoon oyster sauce
1 tablespoon sugar
2 cups coconut milk
Fresh basil leaves for garnish

In a saucepan, heat oil over medium heat. Stir-fry Panang curry paste for 1 minute. Add tenderloin, bell pepper, carrots, fish sauce, oyster sauce, and sugar. Stir-fry for 1 minute, then add coconut milk. Cook until meat is done and coconut milk is reduced by half.

Garnish with fresh basil leaves.

SERVES 2

NOTE: *Panang curry paste, fish sauce, and oyster sauce can be found at Asian markets and well-stocked grocery stores.*

Approximate values per serving: 745 calories, 63 grams fat, 82 milligrams cholesterol, 24 grams carbohydrate, 480 milligrams sodium, 74 percent of calories from fat.

STEAK DIANE

The Arizona Club

PHOENIX AND SCOTTSDALE, ARIZONA

Scott Tompkins, Chef

THE AROMA of this outstanding steak dish is marvelous, and the taste—with its seasoned juices—is fabulous.

> *8 tablespoons butter*
> *Two 3½-ounce tournedos of beef*
> *4 mushrooms, sliced*
> *1 tablespoon thinly sliced shallot*
> *1 clove garlic, minced*
> *1 tablespoon brandy*
> *1 tablespoon Dijon mustard*
> *1 tablespoon red wine*
> *¼ cup demi-glace or beef base*

Melt 4 tablespoons of the butter in a large skillet over high heat. Add tournedos and brown. Add mushrooms and shallot and sauté. Add garlic. Add the brandy, heat until very warm, then carefully ignite it with a match placed at the edge of the pan (the flaming can be skipped if necessary but add the brandy.) Add mustard and wine. Add demi-glace or beef base and reduce liquid by half. Add the remaining 4 tablespoons butter and let melt.

Serve immediately.

SERVES 2

NOTE: *Demi-glace, new to supermarkets but used often by chefs, is a thick paste or granules to which you usually add water. Look for it in the broth and soup area.*

Approximate values per serving: 581 calories, 51 grams fat, 180 milligrams cholesterol, 4 grams carbohydrate, 761 milligrams sodium, 81 percent of calories from fat.

BEAVER STREET BURGERS

The Beaver Street Brewery and Whistle Stop Cafe
FLAGSTAFF, ARIZONA

Kate Chadwick, Chef

THE MOUTHWATERING BEAVER STREET BURGER is one of this chef's many award-winning creations.

2 cups boiling water

⅔ cup sun-dried tomatoes

4 pounds beef chuck roast or ground chuck

2 tablespoons fresh basil leaves, finely chopped

2 tablespoons minced fresh garlic

2 teaspoons kosher salt

1 tablespoon freshly ground black pepper

8 slices Havarti cheese

Basil Pesto Mayonnaise (recipe follows)

8 leaves romaine lettuce

8 slices red onion

8 French rolls

Pour about 2 cups boiling water over the dried tomatoes to reconstitute. Cover and soak until the tomatoes are soft, about 30 minutes. Drain off the remaining water, reserving 2 tablespoons of the tomato "liquor," and chop tomatoes.

If using beef chuck roast, cut meat into 1-inch strips. Grind in a meat grinder using the biggest hole grinder plate (⅜ inch).

Preheat a grill.

In a medium bowl, combine the ground chuck or ground beef, basil, garlic, reconstituted tomatoes, salt, pepper, and sun-dried tomato liquor. Combine well and grind using the smallest hole on the grinder plate and form into eight patties.

Grill over hot coals to desired doneness and serve with sliced Havarti cheese, Basil Pesto Mayonnaise, lettuce, onion slices, and crusty French rolls.

SERVES 8

NOTE: *Chef Chadwick recommends the use of a meat grinder, but similar results can be achieved using ground chuck.*

BASIL PESTO MAYONNAISE

¼ cup mayonnaise
2 tablespoons good-quality basil pesto

Combine mayonnaise and pesto well.

MAKES ¼ CUP

Approximate values per serving: 887 calories, 61 grams total fat, 168 milligrams cholesterol, 36 grams carbohydrate, 1,219 milligrams sodium, 62 percent of calories from fat.

SOUTHWESTERN MEATLOAF

Treet's Deli at A. J.'s Fine Foods

PHOENIX, ARIZONA

Ernie Muniz, Chef

TELL YOUR FAMILY it's meatloaf for dinner and you may hear groans and grumbles. Serve them this meatloaf and they'll clean their plates. Chef Ernie Muniz adds a dash of cayenne, some picante sauce, and Southwest Seasoning's Ajo Picante seasoning (which can be found at A. J.'s) to turn ho-hum meatloaf into a fiesta. This also makes great sandwiches the next day.

2 pounds lean ground beef

¼ cup chopped onion

2 tablespoons chopped green bell pepper

1 clove garlic, chopped

1 teaspoon salt

Dash of cayenne

½ cup frozen whole-kernel corn

2 green onions, chopped

1 teaspoon Ajo Picante seasoning

½ cup plain bread crumbs

2 eggs, beaten

½ cup Pace picante sauce

2½ tablespoons chopped green chiles

1 cup Monterey jack cheese, shredded

¼ cup sliced black olives

1 cup chili sauce

Preheat oven to 350 degrees.

In a large bowl, combine all ingredients. Mix well with your hands. Place into a greased 9 x 5-inch loaf pan and cover with aluminum foil. Bake for 1 to 1½ hours, until meat is no longer pink and juices run clear.

SERVES 8

Approximate values per serving: 449 calories, 32 grams fat, 151 milligrams cholesterol, 13 grams carbohydrate, 747 milligrams sodium, 64 percent of calories from fat.

POULTRY

AZTEC CHICKEN

Beeloe's Cafe

TEMPE, ARIZONA

Randy Barnett, Executive Chef

TRY THIS CHICKEN for a splendid, in-a-hurry company dish that is impressive in appearance and flavor.

Two 4-ounce skinless, boneless chicken breast halves
¾ cup frozen chopped spinach, thawed and squeezed dry
2 tablespoons canned, chopped green chiles
½ cup shredded mixed cheeses, any kind
2 tablespoons cream cheese
¼ teaspoon salt
2 tablespoons melted butter
Salt and pepper to taste
Chipotle Lime Sauce (recipe follows)

Preheat oven to 350 degrees.

Lightly pound chicken flat and set aside. In a small bowl, combine spinach, green chiles, shredded cheeses, cream cheese, and salt. Place half of the mixture in the middle of each breast and roll up neatly.

Place chicken rolls seam side down on a greased sheet pan. Brush with melted butter and season with salt and pepper. Bake until juices run clear, about 15 minutes. Let stand 10 minutes before slicing. Serve with Chipotle Lime Sauce.

SERVES 2

CHIPOTLE LIME SAUCE

1 teaspoon chopped shallot
¼ teaspoon chopped garlic
1 teaspoon chopped chipotle pepper
1 teaspoon fresh lime juice
1 cup heavy cream
½ teaspoon chicken base or bouillon
½ teaspoon cornstarch
1 teaspoon cold water

Process shallot, garlic, chipotle pepper, and lime juice in a food processor until smooth. Place in a small saucepan and add cream and chicken base. Bring to a boil, stirring frequently. In a small dish, mix cornstarch and cold water. Add to cream mixture and simmer 1 minute.

MAKES ABOUT 1 CUP

Approximate values per serving: 726 calories, 60 grams fat, 274 milligrams cholesterol, 9 grams carbohydrate, 888 milligrams sodium, 75 percent of calories from fat.

CHICKEN YUCATAN

Cantina del Pedregal
CAREFREE, ARIZONA

Priscilla Cueto, Chef

COMBINING MANY OF the flavors of the Southwest, this savory chicken dish will quickly become a family and company favorite.

1½ pounds skinless, boneless chicken
½ pound mushrooms, sliced
½ medium onion, diced

2 cloves garlic, minced

2 tablespoons oil

2 cups milk

1 tablespoon chili powder

1½ teaspoons black pepper

1½ teaspoons ground cumin

½ teaspoon cayenne

1 tablespoon salt

2 ounces diced green chiles (one-half of a 4-ounce can)

5⅓ tablespoons butter, melted

½ cup flour, plus extra for dredging

2 cups grated pepper jack cheese

Ten 10-inch flour tortillas

1 egg, beaten

¼ cup cream

Vegetable oil for frying

Boil and shred chicken. Set aside.

In a large skillet, sauté mushrooms, onion, and garlic in oil until soft. Add milk, chili powder, black pepper, cumin, cayenne, salt, and chiles; simmer 10 minutes. Make a roux of melted butter and ½ cup flour; add to skillet and stir until mixture is smooth and thick. Stir in cheese and chicken. Adjust seasoning to taste.

When mixture is cool, wrap about 1 cup into each tortilla. Combine egg and cream in a bowl. Cut tortillas in half on the diagonal, then dip into egg-cream batter. Gently roll tortillas in flour to cover and fry in vegetable oil at 350 degrees until golden brown. Serve immediately.

SERVES 10

Approximate values per serving: 571 calories, 34 grams fat, 134 milligrams cholesterol, 33 grams carbohydrate, 1,123 milligrams sodium, 54 percent of calories from fat.

INDIAN BEND (PUMPKIN RISOTTO)

Sprouts Restaurant at Marriott's Camelback Inn Resort
SCOTTSDALE, ARIZONA

Gary Scherer, Executive Chef

INDIAN BEND, OR Pumpkin Risotto, the unique dish with an equally unique name, adds a delicious twist to a holiday meal.

> *3 cups vegetable stock*
> *2 tablespoons diced yellow onion*
> *2½ tablespoons minced shallot*
> *Dash of olive oil*
> *⅛ teaspoon chopped roasted garlic (for roasting instructions,*
> *   see page 9)*
> *1 cup uncooked arborio rice*
> *¼ cup Pumpkin Purée (recipe follows), or canned pumpkin*
> *¼ cup (2 ounces) smoked chicken (diced small)*
> *2 tablespoons tomatoes (diced small)*
> *1 tablespoon chopped fresh parsley*
> *Parmesan Crisp for garnish (recipe follows)*

Place vegetable stock in a medium saucepan and bring to a simmer. In another medium saucepan, heat onion and shallot in olive oil over medium heat until they begin to turn translucent, about 2 to 3 minutes. Add garlic and rice and stir well. Cook for 5 minutes or until rice is slightly toasted. Slowly add enough hot vegetable stock to just barely cover the rice. Cook and stir continually until stock is absorbed. Continue cooking, adding more stock a bit at a time until two cups have been used. Combine Pumpkin Purée, diced chicken, diced tomatoes, and parsley and add to pot. Continue adding the remaining 1 cup stock and adjust seasoning if needed. The rice is done when it is tender, yet firm to the bite (al dente). It will appear creamy and moist. Serve at once in a pasta bowl and garnish with Parmesan Crisp.

SERVES 2

NOTE: *For instructions on roasting garlic, see page 10.*

PUMPKIN PURÉE

> *1 medium pie pumpkin (about 3 pounds)*
> *¼ teaspoon ground nutmeg*
> *¼ teaspoon ground cinnamon*
> *¼ cup vegetable stock, warmed*
> *Salt and white pepper to taste*

Preheat oven to 325 degrees.

Rinse pumpkin and cut into halves. Place cut side down in a pan with deep sides and cook until soft but not mushy, approximately 45 minutes. When cool enough to handle, remove seeds and scrape out the flesh of the pumpkin with a spoon or fork. Combine with nutmeg and cinnamon in a blender and purée until smooth, adding warm vegetable stock to adjust consistency. Season with salt and white pepper to taste.

MAKES ABOUT 2 CUPS

PARMESAN CRISP

> *1½ tablespoons Parmesan cheese, freshly grated*

Preheat oven to 350 degrees. Thinly spread cheese on a sheet pan. Place in oven until cheese is fully melted and turning slightly brown, about 3 to 5 minutes.

MAKES ABOUT 1½ TABLESPOONS

Approximate values per serving: 708 calories, 13 grams fat, 27 milligrams cholesterol, 122 grams carbohydrate, 2,587 milligrams sodium, 17 percent of calories from fat.

CHICKEN GEORGE

Greektown

PHOENIX, ARIZONA

George Vassiliou, Owner

FRESH DILL, PARSLEY, and Greek oregano lend a fragrant and flavorful touch to this signature dish. It will delight your senses.

2 tablespoons chopped red onion
1 small clove garlic
4 cups homemade chicken stock or broth
1 egg, beaten
6 tablespoons fresh lemon juice
2 tablespoons flour
8 tablespoons butter or margarine
1 teapoon cornstarch
2 tablespoons canola oil
4 skinless, boneless chicken breast halves
8 artichoke hearts, halved
1⅓ cups white wine
Salt and pepper to taste
½ teaspoon Greek oregano
½ teaspoon fresh dill
½ teaspoon fresh parsley
8 large mushrooms, sliced

Purée red onion and garlic together; set aside.

To homemade stock, add egg and lemon juice. Combine flour, margarine or butter, and cornstarch to form a roux. Add roux to stock to thicken to cream-soup consistency.

Heat canola oil in a large, deep skillet over medium heat.

Sauté chicken on both sides until almost done, about 5 minutes. Add remaining 4 tablespoons of butter or margarine, artichoke hearts, wine, stock, puréed onion-garlic mixture, salt and pepper, oregano, dill, and parsley. Simmer 5 minutes, then add mushrooms and simmer 5 to 10 minutes more, until chicken is fully cooked. Serve at once.

SERVES 4

Approximate values per serving: 605 calories, 30 grams fat, 129 milligrams cholesterol, 23 grams carbohydrate, 1,262 milligrams sodium, 47 percent of calories from fat.

ORANGE CHICKEN

The Bamboo Club

PHOENIX AND SCOTTSDALE, ARIZONA

Debbie Bloy, Owner

THE END RESULT of this spicy dish is great, and it cooks quickly. Chili sauce gives it quite a kick, and fresh orange peel lends a tantalizing aroma.

2 cups vegetable oil

1 pound skinless, boneless chicken breast, sliced

2 egg whites, beaten

Salt and pepper to taste

½ cup cornstarch

1 cup flour

1 orange, plus orange slices for garnish

½ onion, chopped

¼ cup chicken stock

4 tablespoons dark soy sauce

2 tablespoons brown sugar

¼ cup tomato sauce

1 tablespoon chili sauce

Heat oil to 375 degrees in a wok.

In a medium bowl, mix chicken with egg whites, salt, and pepper. In a separate bowl, mix together the cornstarch and flour. Dust chicken strips with the mixture, shaking off the excess. Deep-fry chicken in the wok, scattering the pieces with a wooden spatula so the strips do not stick together. When golden brown, set aside chicken and discard the oil. (Do not clean the wok.)

Using a sharp knife, remove orange peel from the orange, being careful not to cut into the white pith. Cut the peel into matchstick-size strips. Extract the juice from the orange (about ½ cup) and set aside. Add onion and orange peel to the wok and stir-fry for two minutes. Add the orange juice, stock, soy sauce, sugar, tomato sauce, and chili sauce and cook on high heat until the sauce is reduced by half, about 2 minutes. Return the chicken to the wok and mix with the sauce, stirring well. Garnish with orange slices.

SERVES 4

Approximate values per serving: 500 calories, 29 grams fat, 73 milligrams cholesterol, 31 grams carbohydrate, 1,163 milligrams sodium, 52 percent of calories from fat.

FISH AND SEAFOOD

SEARED AHI TUNA OVER PENNE PASTA

Casey Moore's Oyster House
TEMPE, ARIZONA

Ian Westlake, Executive Chef

THIS RECIPE IS GREAT for when you want to present something especially wonderful. The combination of seared tuna and penne pasta is delightfully delicious.

> *8 ounces penne pasta*
> *2 tablespoons olive oil*
> *2 ahi tuna steaks (6 to 8 ounces each)*
> *⅓ to ½ cup flour for dredging*
> *¼ cup white wine*
> *12 canned artichoke hearts, halved*
> *2 cups canned, sliced apples, drained*
> *2 cups Spicy Orange Ginger Sauce (recipe follows)*
> *1 bunch fresh spinach, washed and stemmed*
> *Orange and lemon slices for garnish*

Cook pasta al dente and keep it hot while preparing rest of dish.

Heat olive oil in a large sauté pan over medium heat. Dredge both sides of each tuna steak in flour and place in pan. Cook tuna 3 to

4 minutes on each side, until no longer pink. Remove from pan and set aside.

Deglaze pan by adding white wine, scraping up any particles stuck to pan. Add artichoke hearts, apples, and Spicy Orange Ginger Sauce. Bring to a boil, stirring occasionally.

Divide penne pasta and spinach between two plates, add tuna steaks, and top with sauce. Garnish with orange and lemon slices.

SERVES 2 GENEROUSLY

SPICY ORANGE GINGER SAUCE

> *2 cups fresh orange juice*
> *1½ tablespoons grated ginger root*
> *2 tablespoons olive oil*
> *1 teaspoon chopped garlic*
> *1½ teaspoons black pepper*
> *⅛ teaspoon salt*
> *¼ cup Dijon mustard*

In a small saucepan over medium heat, combine all ingredients. Cook 15 to 20 minutes, until sauce is reduced by about one-fourth. Stir in mustard and simmer 15 minutes more.

MAKES APPROXIMATELY 2 CUPS

Approximate values per serving: 1,416 calories, 40 grams fat, 65 milligrams cholesterol, 200 grams carbohydrate, 78 grams protein, 1,018 milligrams sodium, 25 percent of calories from fat.

GARLIC PRAWNS WITH PASTA

The Fish Market

PHOENIX, ARIZONA

Dwight Colton, General Manager

THESE PRAWNS are as easy to prepare as they are to enjoy. In minutes you have an elegant entrée. The serving size is quite large, so this recipe will easily serve four.

4 tablespoons garlic butter
2 ounces white wine
16 prawns, tails on, shells removed (16 to 20 prawns to the pound)
Splash of brandy
Splash of sherry
12 ounces linguine, cooked al dente
2 tablespoons garlic purée
2 tablespoons chopped parsley, plus sprigs for garnish
Lemon wedges for garnish

Heat garlic butter and wine in a medium sauté pan over medium heat. Add prawns and cook until undersides turn white. Flip prawns and cook until bottom side is almost opaque. Flambé with brandy. Add a splash of sherry.

Remove prawns and place over linguine in wide-rimmed soup bowls. Return sauce to heat and correct if needed with butter or wine to prevent it from separating. Add garlic and parsley. Pour overprawns and pasta to coat. Garnish each bowl with a lemon wedge and a sprig of parsley.

SERVES 2 TO 4

NOTE: *You may skip the flambé step if you wish, but the chef believes it adds flavor. If you wish to flambé the cooked prawns, add brandy at the appropriate time, heat until very warm, then carefully ignite it with a match placed at the edge of the pan. Stir carefully with a long spoon; flames will die down right away.*

To make garlic butter, boil 1 clove garlic in water for 3 to 4 minutes, drain, and crush well. Cream 4 tablespoons butter unitl light and fluffy. Add garlic and blend thoroughly. Refrigerate until ready to use.

Approximate values per serving: 938 calories, 26 grams fat, 92 milligrams cholesterol, 132 grams carbohydrate, 269 milligrams sodium, 27 percent of calories from fat.

MACADAMIA NUT–CRUSTED MAHIMAHI WITH FRESH FRUIT RELISH

Razz's Restaurant and Bar
SCOTTSDALE, ARIZONA

Erasmo (Razz) Kamnitzer, Chef/Owner

THIS IS A FABULOUS DISH that you will likely make again and again. The accompanying relish is wonderfully sweet and tangy.

> *⅓ cup flour*
> *Salt and pepper to taste*
> *2 eggs, beaten*
> *¾ cup ground macadamia nuts*
> *½ cup bread crumbs, preferably Panko*
> *2 to 3 tablespoons olive oil*
> *Four 6-ounce filets of mahimahi (blood vein removed)*
> *Fresh Fruit Relish (recipe follows)*

Place flour in a medium bowl and season with salt and pepper. Place beaten eggs in a separate bowl; in a third bowl place ground macadamia nuts and bread crumbs. To prepare mahimahi, first roll in seasoned flour, then dip in the beaten egg, then roll in the macadamia-nut mixture.

Heat olive oil in a large skillet over medium heat and fry filets until golden brown in color, about 2 minutes per side. Slice and serve with Fresh Fruit Relish or serve whole on top of the relish.

SERVES 4

Approximate values per serving (without Fresh Fruit Relish): 413 calories, 20 grams fat, 216 milligrams cholesterol, 19 grams carbohydrate, 38 grams protein, 293 milligrams sodium, 45 percent of calories from fat.

FRESH FRUIT RELISH

⅓ cup diced papaya

⅓ cup diced mango

⅓ cup diced pineapple

⅓ cup diced pears

⅓ cup diced star fruit (carambola)

3 tablespoons chopped cilantro

1 tablespoon chopped garlic

3 tablespoons diced onion

3 tablespoons chopped chives

1 cup mixed diced peppers (red, green, poblano, jalapeño)

Salt and pepper to taste

4 tablespoons fresh lime juice (juice of 2 limes)

3 tablespoons olive oil

In a medium bowl, combine all ingredients. Stir well.

MAKES 4 SERVINGS, ABOUT ½ TO ⅔ CUP EACH

Approximate values per serving (relish only): 138 calories, 11 grams fat, no cholesterol, 12 grams carbohydrate, 3 milligrams sodium, 72 percent of calories from fat.

GAME AND PORK

BREAST OF PHEASANT WITH SUN-DRIED CHERRIES AND VANILLA BEAN SAUCE

El Tovar

EL TOVAR HOTEL, GRAND CANYON, ARIZONA

Scott Kidd, Chef

THIS IS SOMETHING SPECIAL—perfect for a festive family holiday gathering—and easier to prepare than it sounds. The smooth sauce is outstanding.

> *6 pheasant breasts*
> *2 tablespoons vegetable oil*
> *2 egg yolks*
> *2 to 3 tablespoons milk or water*
> *Twelve 8-inch cinnamon tortillas*
> *6 ounces sun-dried cherries*
> *Vanilla Bean Sauce (recipe follows)*

In a medium skillet, briefly sauté pheasant breasts in oil to seal outsides. Set aside and cool.

Preheat oven to 350 degrees.

Combine egg yolks and milk or water to make an egg wash. Set aside.

On a large sheet pan, lay each breast on two cinnamon tortillas that overlap each other by an inch. Place 1 ounce of cherries down the center of each breast. Brush with egg wash to seal and roll up like an egg roll. Brush outside with egg wash and bake for 20 to 25 minutes. Top with Vanilla Bean Sauce and serve.

SERVES 6

NOTE: *If cinnamon tortillas are not available, purchase flour tortillas, brush both sides with egg wash (2 egg yolks mixed with 2 to 3 tablespoons milk or water), and roll in cinnamon sugar (combine ½ cup sugar and 1 tablespoon cinnamon).*

VANILLA BEAN SAUCE

1 cup white wine
1 vanilla bean
1 cup heavy cream
1 tablespoon cornstarch mixed with 1 tablespoon water
4 tablespoons butter, sliced

Heat wine and vanilla bean in a saucepan over medium heat until reduced by half, about 2 minutes. Add cream and bring to a boil. Thicken with cornstarch-water mixture. Remove from heat, whisk in butter, and strain to remove vanilla bean.

MAKES 1 CUP

Approximate values per serving: 693 calories, 38 grams fat, 221 milligrams cholesterol, 45 grams carbohydrate, 493 milligrams sodium, 51 percent of calories from fat.

STUFFED PORK TENDERLOIN

Z'Tejas Grill

SCOTTSDALE, ARIZONA

Leo Madrigal, Chef

YOU'LL WANT TO INVITE YOUR FRIENDS over for this full-flavored dish. It takes a bit of work, but the result is very impressive and equally tasty. The Roasted Garlic Cream sauce is heavenly.

1 poblano pepper
2 pounds pork tenderloin, butterflied
¼ cup chorizo, uncooked
¼ cup grated Monterey jack cheese
1 tablespoon grilled white onion
Roasted Garlic Cream (recipe follows)
Sour cream for garnish

Roast poblano pepper by placing on a hot grill and searing on all sides until skin blackens and begins to blister. Wrap in a paper bag to steam for 2 to 3 minutes. Peel skin off and remove seeds. Flatten into a long strip. Set aside.

Place pork tenderloin on a cutting board. Mash together the chorizo, cheese, and onion and form into a tube.

Preheat a grill or a stove burner to hot.

Preheat oven to 400 degrees.

Place chorizo-cheese mixture in center of tenderloin and top with poblano pepper. Using kitchen twine, tie the pork together as close to its original form as possible. Place on a hot grill or a flat pan on the stovetop and sear on all sides.

Place in oven on a sheet pan for approximately 12 minutes and cook until medium. Remove and let cool.

After pork has cooled, cut into medallions, about 5 ounces each. Reduce grill heat and grill medallions (grill must not be too hot or it will scorch the stuffing).

To serve, place 4 medallions on each plate, top with Roasted Garlic Cream and a zigzag of sour cream.

SERVES 4

ROASTED GARLIC CREAM

1 clove roasted garlic (for roasting instructions, see page 9)
2 tablespoons herb butter
1 quart heavy cream
3 ounces chorizo, cooked
1 tablespoon fresh lime juice

In a medium saucepan, sauté one roasted garlic clove in herb butter. Add cream and chorizo; reduce by half. Stir in lime juice.

MAKES ABOUT 2 CUPS

NOTE: *To make herb butter, cream 4 tablespoons butter until light and fluffy. Add ½ to 1 teaspoon dried herbs (any kind) and blend thoroughly. Refrigerate until ready to use.*

Approximate values per serving: 1,227 calories, 122 grams fat, 420 milligrams cholesterol, 12 grams carbohydrate, 667 milligrams sodium, 88 percent of calories from fat.

PASTA

BAKED SPAGHETTI PIE

Sorrento's Italian Kitchen
TEMPE AND MESA, ARIZONA

Jeffrey Bobigian, Chef/Owner

HERE'S A SOLUTION to many menu dilemmas. The rich Italian flavor of this dish has universal appeal—a definite crowd pleaser.

2 pounds spaghetti
2 pounds ricotta cheese
½ cup whole milk
3 eggs, lightly beaten
1 pound ground beef
1 pound spicy Italian sausage
½ cup spaghetti sauce
1 pound provolone cheese, thinly sliced
½ cup Romano cheese, grated

Preheat oven to 475 degrees.
Cook spaghetti al dente.
In a small bowl mix together ricotta, milk, and eggs. Add mixture to cooked spaghetti and stir together. Press compactly and evenly into a 9 x 13 x 2-inch baking pan.
Preheat oven to 475 degrees.
Cook ground beef and sausage in a large skillet. Drain fat, removing as much as possible. Stir in spaghetti sauce. Spread evenly

over spaghetti in pan. Layer slices of provolone over meat, then top with the grated Romano. Bake 20 minutes.

SERVES 12

Approximate values per serving: 848 calories, 46 grams fat, 185 milligrams cholesterol, 62 grams carbohydrate, 831 milligrams sodium, 50 percent of calories from fat.

VEGETABLE LASAGNA

Kohnie's Gourmet Coffee

PHOENIX, ARIZONA

Ellie Kohn, Owner

THIS IS A DELIGHTFUL MEATLESS ENTRÉE everyone will enjoy—a green salad and French bread are all you need to complement this tasty dish.

4 teaspoons diet margarine
4 cups mushrooms, thinly sliced
4 teaspoons olive oil
1½ cups chopped onion
6 cloves garlic, minced
1¾ cups tomato sauce
1½ cups canned Italian tomatoes
1½ teaspoons salt
2 teaspoons dried oregano
2 teaspoons dried basil
½ teaspoon pepper
2 or 3 bay leaves
Two 10-ounce packages frozen spinach, thawed and drained
2 cups part-skim ricotta cheese

1 egg, beaten
8 ounces lasagna noodles, cooked
16 ounces Monterey jack cheese, shredded (about 4 cups)

Heat margarine in a skillet, sauté mushrooms 2 to 3 minutes. Set aside.

In a 3-quart saucepan, heat olive oil and sauté onion until translucent, about 2 minutes. Add garlic and sauté 1 minute, stirring constantly. Add tomato sauce, tomatoes, salt, oregano, basil, pepper, and bay leaves; bring to a boil and simmer 30 minutes. Remove bay leaves.

Combine spinach, ricotta, and egg in a large bowl.

Preheat oven to 350 degrees.

Spread half the sauce mix on the bottom of a 13 x 9 x 12-inch casserole dish. Add half of the noodles lengthwise, overlapping if necessary. Next, spread half of the spinach mixture, top with half of the mushrooms, more sauce, then half of the Monterey jack cheese. Add the rest of the noodles, this time crosswise. Top with the remaining spinach mixture, mushrooms, sauce, and cheese.

Bake 40 to 50 minutes. Let stand 15 minutes before serving.

SERVES 8

Approximate values per serving: 437 calories, 22 grams fat, 87 milligrams cholesterol, 37 grams carbohydrate, 1,109 milligrams sodium, 45 percent of calories from fat.

RED CHILE ANGEL HAIR PASTA

Richardson's

PHOENIX, ARIZONA

Victor M. Romero, Sous Chef

START WITH a simple, superb Alfredo sauce and create a fiesta by combining it with the zesty red chile angel hair pasta. This rich dish makes a satisfying main course or can be served as a side dish.

8 ounces red chile angel hair pasta
2 teaspoons olive oil
2 cloves garlic, minced
2 cups heavy cream
3 to 4 drops lemon juice
1 tablespoon butter
½ cup grated Romano cheese
Salt and pepper to taste

Cook pasta according to package directions.

Heat the olive oil in a small sauté pan over medium heat and sauté the garlic for 1 to 2 minutes. Add cream and lemon juice and bring to a quick boil, stirring occasionally. Reduce heat to medium-low and reduce the cream until it coats the back of a spoon, about 5 minutes. Stir in the butter and the red chile pasta, combining well. Add the Romano and stir until melted. Season with salt and pepper.

SERVES 2

NOTE: *Red chile angel hair pasta can be tricky to find—your best bet is specialty food stores. Red chile fettuccine is sometimes easier to find and is an acceptable substitute, says Chef Romero.*

Approximate values per serving: 1,296 calories, 114 grams fat, 357 milligrams cholesterol, 51 grams carbohydrate, 524 milligrams sodium, 78 percent of calories from fat.

ANGEL HAIR PASTA

Hops! Bistro and Brewery

SCOTTSDALE AND PHOENIX, ARIZONA

Alan Skversky, Executive Chef/General Manager

A PERFECTLY SEASONED DISH of angel hair pasta in a light broth with spinach, mushrooms, and tomatoes, this colorful main course is also superb when served as a side dish.

24 ounces uncooked angel hair pasta
½ cup extra-virgin olive oil
4 teaspoons minced shallot
4 teaspoons minced garlic
1 cup sliced medium-size mushrooms
1 cup oyster mushrooms, stemmed
1 cup diced small Roma tomatoes
12 ounces fresh spinach, washed and stemmed
½ cup white wine
1 cup vegetable broth
Salt and pepper to taste

Cook pasta al dente and keep warm.

Heat olive oil in a small skillet over medium heat. Sauté shallot, garlic, and all mushrooms until soft. Add tomatoes and spinach, then add white wine and mix well. When this begins to simmer, add the broth and season with salt and pepper to taste. Return to a simmer. Toss with angel hair pasta.

SERVES 4 GENEROUSLY

Approximate values per serving: 1,255 calories, 61 grams fat, 1 milligram cholesterol, 146 grams carbohydrate, 466 milligrams sodium, 44 percent of calories from fat.

CANNELLONI

Grandinetti's Pasta House and Bar
PHOENIX, ARIZONA

Mark Farer, Kitchen Manager

KIDS AS WELL AS ADULTS will enjoy this version of a classic dish.

2 pounds lean ground beef
¾ cup chopped yellow onion
2 eggs, lightly beaten
½ cup grated Parmesan cheese
1 cup plain bread crumbs
1½ tablespoons finely chopped garlic
¾ cup flour
Special Seasoning (recipe follows)
16 cooked crepes or manicotti shells
2 cups marinara sauce, or your favorite red sauce, or 2 cups white
 sauce (homemade or your favorite brand)

In a large sauté pan over medium heat, cook ground beef and yellow onions until meat is fully cooked and onions are tender, about 12 to 15 minutes. Add the eggs, Parmesan, bread crumbs, garlic, and flour, mixing together well. Stir in Special Seasoning and reduce heat to low.

Preheat oven to 350 degrees.

If using crepes, place 4 to 5 ounces (about ½ cup) of filling in the center of each crepe and roll lengthwise; if using manicotti shells, gently stuff filling inside shells with a spoon. Place in a 9 x 13-inch pan. (Cannelloni may be frozen at this point or refrigerated until ready to cook. If frozen, thaw in refrigerator overnight before serving.)

Bake, covered, for about 20 minutes.

To serve, place two shells on each plate and top with your favorite red or white sauce.

SERVES 8

NOTE: *Crepes or manicotti shells may be used in this recipe. Crepes are a little easier to handle and can be found ready-made in most grocery stores.*

SPECIAL SEASONING

> *1¼ teaspoons granulated garlic*
> *1¼ teaspoons salt*
> *1¼ teaspoons white pepper*
> *1¼ teaspoons dried basil*

Combine all ingredients.

MAKES 5 TEASPOONS

Approximate values per serving: 619 calories, 29 grams fat, 141 milligrams cholesterol, 55 grams carbohydrate, 867 milligrams sodium, 43 percent of calories from fat.

GRILLED CHICKEN PASTA

Old Town Tortilla Factory

SCOTTSDALE, ARIZONA

Patrick Hughes, Chef

THIS PASTA EXPLODES with the flavors of the Southwest. The roasted corn, cilantro–black bean fettucine, and Red Chile Pesto give this innovative entrée its tantalizing flavor.

> *½ cup Red Chile Pesto (recipe follows)*
> *2 teaspoons olive oil*

1 cup roasted corn
1 cup cooked black beans
1 cup diced tomatoes
1½ cups chicken stock
2½ cups heavy whipping cream
4 skinless, boneless chicken breast halves, grilled and julienned
Salt and pepper to taste
1 pound cilantro–black bean fettucine

Heat olive oil in a large saucepan over medium heat and sauté corn, black beans, and tomatoes for 2 minutes. Add chicken stock and Red Chile Pesto and reduce by half, about 2 minutes. Stir in cream, reduce by half, and add chicken. Season with salt and pepper.

Cook pasta in boiling salted water according to package directions and toss with chicken/cream mixture.

SERVES 4

NOTE: *Though any variety of fettucine may be used, cilantro–black bean fettucine is the essence of this recipe. It can be found in specialty grocery stores.*

Roast corn on the cob over an open grill for 10 to 15 minutes or kernels on a cookie sheet at 400 degrees for 10 to 15 minutes until golden brown.

RED CHILE PESTO

1 ancho chile, roasted (for roasting instructions, see page 12)
2 teaspoons roasted garlic (for roasting instructions, see page 9)
1 red bell pepper, chopped
⅓ cup pine nuts
2 tablespoons lemon juice
⅓ cup olive oil

Combine all ingredients in a food processor and blend until smooth. Set aside for 1 hour, then season to taste.

MAKES 1 CUP

Approximate values per serving: 1,200 calories, 42 grams fat, 255 milligrams cholesterol, 155 grams carbohydrate, 436 milligrams sodium, 31 percent of calories from fat.

SPYROS PASTA

RoxSand Restaurant and Bar

PHOENIX, ARIZONA

RoxSand Suarez Scocos, Owner

WHEN YOU'RE IN THE MOOD for something out of the ordinary, try this recipe. Wild mushrooms and sun-dried tomatoes help make Spyros Pasta an exquisite entrée.

> *1 small red onion, chopped*
> *2 cloves garlic, chopped*
> *2 ounces wild mushrooms (oyster, portabello), sliced*
> *1 tablespoon olive oil*
> *2 ounces sun-dried tomatoes, reconstituted according to*
>   *package directions*
> *¼ cup white wine*
> *½ cup chicken stock*
> *½ cup chopped fresh spinach*
> *2⅔ tablespoons chopped fresh basil*
> *¼ cup plus 2 tablespoons grated Parmesan cheese*
> *Salt and pepper to taste*
> *8 ounces linguine, cooked*

Sauté onion, garlic, and mushrooms in olive oil. Add sun-dried tomatoes. Add white wine to deglaze, scraping any particles from the pan, and reduce until almost dry. Add chicken stock, spinach, basil, cheese, and salt and pepper to taste. Toss with Linguine to serve.

SERVES 4

Approximate values per serving: 310 calories, 7 grams fat, 6 milligrams cholesterol, 48 grams carbohydrate, 530 milligrams sodium, 21 percent of calories from fat.

SPICY CHICKEN AND TOMATO PASTA

Planet Hollywood

PHOENIX, ARIZONA

Diane LaJoie, Chef

THIS FANTASTIC DISH features sautéed chicken, plum tomatoes, fresh basil, and Parmesan cheese tossed with penne pasta. Don't let the calorie count fool you—this recipe can easily serve two or three people.

> ¼ cup herbed olive oil
> 4 ounces skinless, boneless chicken breast, cut into strips
> 1 cup sliced mushrooms
> ½ cup strips of green bell pepper
> ½ cup chopped red onion
> 2½ teaspoons minced garlic
> ⅓ cup chopped plum tomatoes
> 2 tablespoons white wine
> ⅔ cup tomato sauce
> 3½ tablespoons shredded Parmesan cheese
> 2 tablespoons shredded fresh basil
> ¾ teaspoon crushed red pepper flakes
> 8 ounces penne pasta, cooked

Heat olive oil in a large skillet over medium heat. Cook chicken strips and mushrooms for 3 minutes. Add bell pepper, onion, and garlic. Toss well. Add tomatoes and toss. Remove chicken mixture from pan and keep warm.

Add white wine to pan to deglaze and scrape up any bits left clinging from the chicken mixture. Add tomato sauce, 2 tablespoons of the Parmesan, basil, and red pepper flakes. Add cooked pasta to pan and mix well with the sauce. Place chicken and pasta mixture in a large pasta bowl. Sprinkle with remaining 1½ tablespoons Parmesan cheese.

MAKES 1 GENEROUS SERVING

NOTE: *Look for herbed olive oil in well-stocked grocery stores or specialty food stores.*

Approximate values per serving (for one restaurant serving, ample food for at least two or three people): 1,583 calories, 54 grams fat, 80 milligrams cholesterol, 201 grams carbohydrate, 1,462 milligrams sodium, 31 percent of calories from fat.

*V*EGETARIAN

*V*EGETARIAN *B*LACK *B*EANS

Chevy's Mexican Restaurant

PHOENIX, ARIZONA

THE REQUESTS HAVE POURED IN for this delicious recipe. In addition to the great taste of black beans, they are an excellent source of virtually fat-free protein. Enjoy them in this recipe with a south-of-the-border flair.

1 tablespoon canola oil
½ cup onion, diced
1 clove garlic, chopped
5 cups water
2 tablespoons powdered vegetable-soup base
2 tablespoons tomato paste
4 ounces Dos Equis beer
1½ teaspoons pepper
½ pound dried black beans, rinsed
1¼ teaspoons epazote
1½ teaspoons chopped fresh cilantro
1 tablespoon chili powder
1 tablespoon ground cumin

Heat canola oil in a large stockpot over medium heat. Sauté onions and garlic for 5 minutes. Add water, soup base, tomato paste, beer, and pepper; bring to a boil. Add beans and reduce to a simmer.

Simmer for 3 hours, stirring occasionally. Add epazote, cilantro, chili powder, and cumin; simmer for 10 minutes more. Beans should be soft but firm and have a thick, gravylike consistency.

SERVES 8

NOTE: *Epazote, a pungent wild herb with a taste similar to that of fresh coriander, can be found in well-stocked grocery stores or in Latin markets. Look for vegetable-soup base in the seasonings sections of supermarkets.*

Approximate values per serving: 165 calories, 3 grams fat, no cholesterol, 26 grams carbohydrate, 605 milligrams sodium, 18 percent of calories from fat.

VEGETABLE BURRITOS

Hops! Bistro and Brewery

SCOTTSDALE AND PHOENIX, ARIZONA

Alan Skversky, Executive Chef/General Manager

ONE OF THE MOST DELICIOUS meatless dishes you'll ever try is this burrito. Stuffed with lightly sautéed vegetables and rice, it is a great (and easy) dish to serve to a large crowd.

Along with the Jicama Coleslaw, you might serve this with salsa, pico de gallo, and black beans.

> *2½ tablespoons olive oil*
> *1½ cups broccoli florets*
> *⅔ cup roasted and diced red bell pepper (for roasting instructions, see page 12)*
> *2 green chiles, cut into strips*
> *2½ cups diced zucchini*
> *2½ cups diced yellow squash*
> *5 cups quartered button mushrooms*
> *2¼ cups fresh spinach, rinsed*
> *1⅔ cups cooked white rice*
> *½ teaspoon salt*
> *1½ teaspoons pepper*
> *6 flour tortillas*
> *6 ounces Sonoma jack cheese, sliced*
> *Jicama Coleslaw (recipe follows)*

Heat olive oil in a large skillet over medium heat. Sauté broccoli, roasted pepper, green chiles, zucchini, yellow squash, and mushrooms in olive oil until barely tender, about 3 to 5 minutes. Stir in spinach, rice, salt, and pepper and continue to cook 3 minutes more. Wrap mixture in tortillas and top each with a slice of cheese. Warm burritos in microwave before serving to melt the cheese.

Serve with Jicama Coleslaw, salsa, pico de gallo, and black beans.

SERVES 6

Approximate values per serving (without coleslaw): 393 calories, 17 grams fat, 25 milligrams cholesterol, 772 milligrams sodium, 46 grams carbohydrate, 39 percent of calories from fat.

JICAMA COLESLAW

1⅔ cups julienned jicama

⅓ cup julienned green bell pepper

⅓ cup julienned red bell pepper

¼ cup julienned zucchini

¼ cup julienned yellow squash

½ cup julienned carrots

½ cup rice vinegar

2 tablespoons lime juice

⅛ teaspoon sugar

½ teaspoon kosher salt

1 teaspoon pepper

Combine the jicama, bell peppers, zucchini, squash, and carrots in a medium bowl and set aside. In a separate bowl, combine the vinegar, lime juice, sugar, salt, and pepper. Pour over vegetables and toss until all ingredients are coated evenly.

MAKES ABOUT 3½ CUPS

Approximate values per serving (about ½ cup of coleslaw): 28 calories, less than 1 gram fat, no cholesterol, 139 milligrams sodium, 7 grams carbohydrate, 3 percent of calories from fat.

VEGETARIAN BLACK BEAN CHILI

Bean Tree Coffee House

PHOENIX, ARIZONA

Craig Szczepkowski, Chef

THIS CHILI IS a delicious meatless alternative and is great for buffet suppers or parties after the game.

1 to 2 tablespoons olive oil
2 onions, diced
4 cloves garlic, minced
2 bay leaves
½ teaspoon ground cumin
1 teaspoon dried oregano
1 tablespoon paprika
½ teaspoon cayenne
1 tablespoon chili powder
½ teaspoon salt
30 ounces diced tomatoes (about 4⅛ cups), including juice
2½ cups dried black beans, soaked overnight in just enough
  water to cover
Water or vegetable broth for rehydrating
1 tablespoon rice wine vinegar

In a large stockpot, heat the olive oil over medium heat and add onions and garlic. Sauté until the onions just begin to caramelize, about 10 minutes. Reduce heat to medium, add bay leaves, cumin, oregano, paprika, cayenne, chili powder, and salt and cook 1 minute longer, stirring constantly so spices do not stick and burn.

Add tomatoes and black beans. Reduce heat to low and simmer for 1½ hours, stirring occasionally to prevent scorching. Add water or vegetable broth as needed if soup starts to dry out. Stir in rice wine vinegar and serve.

SERVES 12 AS AN APPETIZER, 6 TO 8 AS A MAIN COURSE

Approximate values per serving (based on 6 servings): 780 calories, 6 grams fat, no cholesterol, 140 grams carbohydrate, 1,217 milligrams sodium, 7 percent of calories from fat.

FOUL MAUDAMMAS

La Mediterraneé de Sedona
SEDONA, ARIZONA

Antoine Hanna

IMPRESS YOUR GUESTS with this first-prize winner of the Arizona Garlic Festival. Foul Maudammas, or marinated fava beans, is an outstanding dish. It's also easy to prepare and makes an attractive presentation.

> 5½ cups dried fava beans
> ⅔ cup olive oil
> 6 tablespoons crushed garlic
> 1½ cups yellow onions, diced small (about 2 medium)
> 1½ cups green bell pepper, diced small (about 2 medium)
> 1½ cups tomato, diced small (about 2 medium)
> Juice of 4 lemons
> Salt and pepper to taste
> Fresh mint and fresh parsley for garnish

Soak beans in water overnight. The next morning, drain and cover with fresh water in a large pan. Bring to a boil, cover, and simmer until beans are tender, about 30 minutes.

In a medium bowl, stir together olive oil and garlic. Add onion, green pepper, and tomato.

Drain the beans, leaving only a small amount of water. Mash half the beans, leaving the rest whole. Add vegetables, lemon juice, and salt and pepper, mixing well. Garnish with mint and parsley. Serve warm or cold.

SERVES 4

NOTE: *Dried fava beans are available at Middle Eastern grocery stores.*

Approximate values per serving: 485 calories, 39 grams fat, no cholesterol, 28 grams carbohydrate, 221 milligrams sodium, 70 percent of calories from fat.

EGGPLANT PARMIGIANA

Maria's When In Naples
SCOTTSDALE, ARIZONA

Raul Cisneros, Chef

THIS HEARTY VEGETARIAN eggplant parmigiana is a great winter's night dish and a splendid alternative to lasagna. Chef Cisneros recommends using your own homemade marinara sauce in this recipe but says better-quality store-bought brands work well, too.

> *2 large eggplants (1 pound each)*
> *1 cup flour*
> *4 eggs*
> *⅓ cup milk*
> *Salt and pepper to taste*
> *1½ cups vegetable oil*
> *1 quart marinara sauce*

4 ounces ricotta cheese (about ½ cup)
6 ounces shredded mozzarella cheese (about 1½ cups)
3 ounces grated Parmesan cheese (about 1 cup)
Chopped dried parsley and basil, to taste

Preheat oven to 375 degrees.

Peel the eggplant and slice lengthwise into ¼-inch slices. Dust the eggplant slices with flour.

In a bowl, beat together eggs, milk, salt, and pepper. Dip and coat the floured slices and fry in oil until golden brown on both sides. Blot both sides of slices with paper towels to remove excess oil.

Moisten the bottom of a large casserole dish with marinara sauce, then layer accordingly: eggplant; a thin layer of ricotta, mozzarella, and Parmesan; parsley, basil, salt, and pepper. Repeat layers.

Cover the top layer with remaining marinara sauce and cheeses. Bake for 12 to 15 minutes.

SERVES 5

Approximate values per serving: 623 calories, 41 grams fat, 143 milligrams cholesterol, 44 grams carbohydrate, 1,774 milligrams sodium, 57 percent of calories from fat.

BREADS AND MUFFINS

SPICERY ROLLS

The Spicery

GLENDALE, ARIZONA

Martha Campbell, Chef/Owner

THESE ROLLS ARE UNLIKE MOST yeast breads you may have come across, but they are airy and light, fragrant and irresistible. You may also make small loaves of bread instead of rolls.

1½ cups boiling water
½ cup margarine
1½ teaspoons salt
1 cup sugar
1½ cups additional water (not boiling)
6 ounces (¾ cup) evaporated milk
¼ cup active dry yeast
9⅛ cups flour
Vegetable oil for oiling large bowl

In a large bowl, pour boiling water over margarine. Add salt and sugar; stir well. When margarine is melted, mix in additional water. Stir in evaporated milk and yeast. Let bubble. Slowly add flour.

Turn out on a floured board and knead about 10 minutes. Next, oil a large bowl thoroughly, place the dough in it, and turn it over so the entire surface is oiled. Let rise in a warm place until doubled, punching down twice; about 1 hour. Form into dinner-size rolls. Let rise until doubled while preheating oven to 375 degrees.

Bake for 20 minutes.

MAKES 36 ROLLS

Approximate values per serving: 169 calories, 3 grams fat, 1 milligram cholesterol, 38 grams carbohydrate, 126 milligrams sodium, 17 percent of calories from fat.

CRANBERRY MUFFINS

Fuego Restaurant at the Doubletree Paradise Valley Resort

SCOTTSDALE, ARIZONA

Michael O'Dowd, Executive Chef

THESE MUFFINS ARE FULL of vibrant flavor and are low in fat, just 3 grams apiece. Plain yogurt replaces some of the butter to help make them moist.

2 cups flour
1 cup sugar
1 teaspoon baking powder
1 teaspoon baking soda
½ teaspoon salt
½ cup plain yogurt
⅓ cup orange juice
4 tablespoons melted butter
1 egg
1½ teaspoons vanilla extract
¼ teaspoon grated orange rind
2 cups fresh cranberries, coarsely chopped

Preheat oven to 400 degrees.

In a large bowl, sift together the flour, sugar, baking powder, baking soda, and salt. In a separate bowl, mix together yogurt, orange juice, butter, egg, vanilla extract, and orange rind. Blend together dry and liquid ingredients by hand until all ingredients are just moist. Fold in chopped cranberries.

Pour into greased or paper-lined muffin tins, three-fourths full. Bake for 18 to 22 minutes.

MAKES 18 TO 24 MUFFINS

Approximate values per serving (based on 18 muffins): 132 calories, 3 grams fat, 19 milligrams cholesterol, 24 grams carbohydrate, 182 mg sodium, 22 percent of calories from fat.

OLD-FASHIONED LEMON BREAD

Bean Tree Coffee House

PHOENIX, ARIZONA

Craig Szczepkowski, Chef

THIS SCRUMPTIOUS TREAT can be prepared in about ten minutes and is perfect with brunch or afternoon tea.

1½ cups flour
1⅓ cup sugar
1 teaspoon baking powder
½ teaspoon salt
2 eggs
½ cup whole milk
½ cup vegetable oil
2 teaspoons grated lemon peel
¼ cup lemon juice

Preheat oven to 350 degrees and lightly grease an 8 x 5-inch loaf pan.

In a medium bowl, combine the flour, 1 cup of the sugar, baking powder, and salt. In another medium bowl, whisk together the eggs, milk, oil, and lemon peel. Add the dry ingredients to the liquid ingredients and stir just enough to moisten the mixture. Pour into prepared loaf pan and bake 40 to 45 minutes or until bread is golden. Let cool about 10 minutes and poke holes with a wooden skewer about 1 inch deep on top of bread.

To make the glaze, dissolve remaining ⅓ cup of sugar in lemon juice in a small saucepan over medium-low heat, stirring constantly. Drizzle glaze over bread and let cool before serving.

MAKES 12 SLICES

Approximate values per slice: 242 calories, 10 grams fat, 32 milligrams cholesterol, 35 grams carbohydrate, 3 grams protein, 134 milligrams sodium, 38 percent of calories from fat.

DRIED CHERRY SCONES

The Phoenician

SCOTTSDALE, ARIZONA

Richard Ruskell, Pastry Chef

GOING TO THE PHOENICIAN for tea is a favorite pastime of many Valley residents. And what could go better with a steaming cup of tea than these scones? These treats are heavenly when spread with jam and butter, or plain, fresh from the oven.

1½ cups dried cherries
5 cups cake flour
Pinch of salt
2 tablespoons plus 2 teaspoons baking powder
1 tablespoon ground nutmeg
12 tablespoons butter, sliced
⅛ cup sugar
1 cup plus ¼ cup milk
2 eggs

Preheat oven to 375 degrees. Place the cherries in a small bowl with enough cold water to cover (about 1 cup) and allow to soak while you prepare the remaining ingredients.

Sift the cake flour, salt, baking powder, and nutmeg in a large mixing bowl. Using a pastry blender, cut the butter into the flour mixture until the mixture has a fine texture. Make a well in the center of the butter-flour mixture and add the sugar, 1 cup milk, and 1 egg. Gradually mix either by hand or with an electric mixer into a medium-firm dough. Do not overmix as this will toughen the dough.

Preheat oven to 375 degrees.

Thoroughly drain all water from the cherries, then fold them into the dough. On a floured surface, roll dough to a ⅝-inch thickness and cut into six 4-inch circles. (A large plastic cup works well as a cutter.) Cut each circle of dough into quarters. Place the dough quarters on a lightly greased baking sheet.

Beat together remaining egg and ¼ cup milk. Brush dough quarters with egg wash. Allow to stand approximately 15 minutes before baking.

Bake for 12 to 15 minutes or until golden brown.

MAKES 24 SCONES

Approximate values per serving: 169 calories, 7 grams fat, 35 milligrams cholesterol, 24 grams carbohydrate, 198 milligrams sodium, 36 percent of calories from fat.

PEPPER-CORN MUFFINS

Sandolo Restaurant at the Hyatt Regency Scottsdale at Gainey Ranch

SCOTTSDALE, ARIZONA

Anton Brunbauer, Executive Chef

SERVED WITH A BIG BOWL OF SPICY CHILI or a hearty soup, these Cheddar and chile pepper muffins are all you need to round out a meal.

1 tablespoon olive oil
1 yellow onion, finely chopped
½ green bell pepper, finely chopped
¼ red bell pepper, finely chopped
½ green chile, finely chopped
2 tablespoons butter
¼ cup sugar
1 egg

1 cup bread flour, sifted
1 tablespoon baking powder
1½ teaspoons baking soda
1 teaspoon salt
1 cup cornmeal
½ cup milk
5 ounces grated Cheddar cheese
¾ cup grated Parmesan cheese

Preheat oven to 350 degrees. Grease muffin tins for 18 muffins or line with paper liners.

Heat olive oil in a medium sauté pan over medium heat. Sauté chopped onion, bell peppers, and green chile until tender, then drain on paper towels and let cool.

In a medium mixing bowl, cream together butter and sugar. Add egg while continuing to mix. Add flour, baking powder, baking soda, and salt. Stir in cornmeal and milk. Add sautéed vegetables and grated cheeses, stirring until well incorporated. Pour into muffin tins and bake until lightly browned, about 25 minutes.

MAKES 18 MUFFINS

Approximate values per serving: 120 calories, 5 grams fat, 24 milligrams cholesterol, 16 grams carbohydrate, 416 milligrams sodium, 38 percent of calories from fat.

Muffin Mix

NM Cafe at Neiman Marcus
SCOTTSDALE, ARIZONA

Anthony Bespa, General Manager

THIS SUPERB RECIPE has endless possibilities. With this batter tucked away in the refrigerator, it's no trouble to bake a different batch of muffins every day. Toppings such as pecans, blueberries, or cranberries can be added for an extra burst of flavor.

2 teaspoons baking powder
1 teaspoon baking soda
1 teaspoon salt
2½ cups flour
3 eggs
1 cup sugar
1 cup brown sugar
1 cup vegetable oil
1 teaspoon maple extract
1 teaspoon vanilla extract
2 cups shredded zucchini, or 2 cups chopped banana

Preheat oven to 350 degrees.

In a medium mixing bowl, sift together baking powder, baking soda, salt, and flour and set aside. Using an electric mixer set at medium speed, beat eggs, sugars, oil, and extracts together in a medium bowl until smooth. Add zucchini (or bananas) and mix well. Slowly add flour mixture and blend until smooth.

Pour into a greased muffin pan and bake for 18 to 20 minutes.

MAKES 10 TO 12 MUFFINS

NOTE: *This batter can be kept in the refrigerator for up to 2 weeks.*

Approximate values per serving using shredded zucchini (based on 10 muffins): 387 calories, 20 grams fat, 53 milligrams cholesterol, 55 grams carbohydrate, 365 milligrams sodium, 45 percent of calories from fat.

Approximate values per serving using chopped banana (based on 10 muffins): 419 calories, 20 grams fat, 53 milligrams cholesterol, 62 grams carbohydrate, 365 milligrams sodium, 42 percent of calories from fat.

SOUTHWESTERN GREEN CHILE CORN BREAD

Windows on the Green at the Phoenician
SCOTTSDALE, ARIZONA

Judy Capertina, Pastry Chef

THIS MOIST CORNBREAD will surprise you with the delicious taste of sun-dried cherries. It's a wonderful way to perk up a simple supper.

16 tablespoons (1 cup) butter
¾ cup sugar
4 eggs
1 cup flour
1 cup yellow cornmeal
2 tablespoons baking powder
½ cup diced green chiles
1½ cups cream-style corn
½ cup shredded Cheddar cheese
½ cup shredded jack cheese
½ cup finely chopped sun-dried cherries

Preheat oven to 325 degrees.

Generously butter a 9-inch-square pan, or spray cast-iron cornstick pans with a nonstick spray and heat them in the oven for 7 minutes.

Using an electric mixer set at medium speed, cream butter and sugar together in a large mixing bowl until light and fluffy, about 5 minutes. Add eggs one at a time, mixing well after each addition. Slowly add flour, cornmeal, and baking powder. Add green chiles, corn, cheeses, and cherries; mix well.

If using a square pan, pour mixture into pan and bake for approximately 45 to 50 minutes. If using cornstick pans, bake for 10 to 12 minutes. Bread should be golden brown.

SERVES 24

Approximate values per serving: 180 calories, 10 grams fat, 60 milligrams cholesterol, 20 grams carbohydrate, 252 milligrams sodium, 49 percent of calories from fat.

RASPBERRY COFFEECAKE

Razz's Restaurant and Bar

SCOTTSDALE, ARIZONA

Erasmo (Razz) Kamnitzer, Chef/Owner

THIS IS A GRAND CHOICE for a special brunch or a leisurely weekend breakfast. Sour cream helps make the cake moist, and the raspberry filling adds a delicious twist.

1 cup sugar
½ teaspoon cinnamon
⅔ cup raspberries (preferably fresh)
8 tablespoons butter, softened, plus some to coat Bundt pan
¼ cup brown sugar
2 eggs
1¼ cups sour cream
¾ teaspoon baking powder
¾ teaspoon baking soda
1 teaspoon vanilla
2 cups flour, plus some to dust Bundt pan
2 ounces (about ½ cup) chopped nuts (your choice)

Preheat oven to 350 degrees.

Mix together sugar, cinnamon, and raspberries in a small bowl. Set aside.

In a large mixing bowl, use an electric mixer set at medium speed to cream together 8 tablespoons of the butter and the sugar until fluffy. Add eggs, mix for 2 minutes, then fold in sour cream. Add baking powder, baking soda, and vanilla and mix for 1 minute more. Add flour and mix for about 15 seconds to barely incorporate (do not overmix). Fold in chopped nuts.

Coat a Bundt pan with butter and dust with flour. Add half the dough mixture to the cake pan. Add a layer of raspberry filling. Add the rest of the cake batter on top. Bake for approximately 45 to 50 minutes or until done.

MAKES 10 SERVINGS

Approximate values per serving: 376 calories, 20 grams fat, 80 milligrams cholesterol, 46 grams carbohydrate, 246 milligrams sodium, 46 percent of calories from fat.

SQUAW BREAD

The Chart House

SCOTTSDALE, ARIZONA

Rick Gamboa, Manager

THIS IS A HEARTY, HEALTHY, FLAVORFUL BREAD with just 1 gram of fat per slice. Made with rolled oats, granola, oat bran, and a touch of molasses, it is wonderful even without butter or jam.

1½ cups water
¼ cup dark molasses
2¾ cups flour
¾ cup whole wheat flour

1 package (¼-ounce) active dry yeast
¾ cup bran
½ cup dark brown sugar
⅛ cup oat bran
⅛ cup rolled oats
2 teaspoons dry malt
2 teaspoons salt
1 tablespoon granola
Parchment paper

In a large mixing bowl, combine water and molasses. Mix with a wooden spoon until blended. In a separate bowl, combine the flours and yeast until well blended. Add yeast mixture to the molasses mixture and stir for 2 minutes with a wooden spoon. Add the bran, sugar, oat bran, rolled oats, malt, salt, and granola, stirring well.

Knead dough for 8 minutes on a floured board, then flatten dough to a 12-inch circle. Roll up in a jelly-roll fashion and seal seam completely by pinching dough. Gently place dough on a sheet pan lined with parchment paper. Cover and place in a warm area to rise for 45 to 50 minutes. The loaf should double in size.

Preheat oven to 375 degrees. Score top of loaf three times with a very sharp knife and sprinkle with water.

Bake 50 minutes until the top is light brown.

MAKES 1 LOAF

NOTE: *Some ingredients may be hard to find—check a health-food store for items not found in the grocery store.*

Approximate value per slice: 180 calories, 1 gram fat, no cholesterol, 40 grams carbohydrate, 258 milligrams sodium, 4 percent of calories from fat.

Desserts

COOKIE PIE

Hops! Bistro and Brewery
SCOTTSDALE AND PHOENIX, ARIZONA

Alan Skversky, Executive Chef/General Manager

THIS SCRUMPTIOUS PIE is a simple yet delightfully different treat. The entire family will love it.

> 1 cup (2 sticks) unsalted butter
> 3 cups dark brown sugar
> 2 extra-large eggs
> 1½ teaspoons vanilla extract
> 5 cups flour
> 1 teaspoon baking soda
> 1 cup semisweet chocolate chips
> ⅔ cup white chocolate chips
> ½ cup pecan pieces
> ½ cup coarsely chopped walnuts

Preheat oven to 275 degrees.

Using an electric mixer set at medium speed, in a large bowl, cream butter and sugar until fluffy, then add eggs and vanilla. Slowly add flour and baking soda and mix well. Fold in chocolate chips.

Butter and flour a ten-inch springform pan. Pour nuts into the bottom of the pan and press cookie dough over the nuts. Bake at 275 degrees for approximately 1 hour or until a toothpick inserted in the center comes out almost clean.

SERVES 12

Approximate values per serving: 661 calories, 30 grams fat, 77 milligrams cholesterol, 94 grams carbohydrate, 124 milligrams sodium, 41 percent of calories from fat.

ADOLF'S BUTTER CAKE

The Phoenician

SCOTTSDALE, ARIZONA

Adolf Biewald, Head Baker

THIS MELT-IN-YOUR-MOUTH CAKE will soon become one of your favorites. It is surprisingly easy to make.

3¼ cups flour, plus some for rolling dough
1¼ cups sugar
2 packages active dry yeast
1 cup milk, room temperature
1 egg, room temperature
1 cup (2 sticks) butter
¼ cup ground cinnamon

Preheat oven to 400 degrees.

Place flour and ¼ cup of the sugar in a large mixing bowl. Add yeast, milk, egg, and half the butter. Using an electric mixer, mix dough for 3 to 4 minutes on medium speed until smooth. Let dough rest for 30 minutes.

Dust work surface with flour and roll dough to ¼-inch thickness. Place on a greased cookie sheet.

Take the remaining stick of butter and pinch off small pieces, placing them ½-inch apart on the dough. Let dough rise until doubled in size.

Mix together cinnamon and remaining cup of sugar and cover dough with a heavy sprinkling of the mixture. Bake for 15 to 20 minutes until golden. Let cake cool; cut into 1 x 2-inch pieces.

SERVES 24

Approximate values per serving: 185 calories, 9 grams fat, 31 milligrams cholesterol, 25 grams carbohydrate, 87 milligrams sodium, 41 percent of calories from fat.

Bread Pudding with Warm Whiskey Sauce

Mimi's Cafe

SCOTTSDALE, ARIZONA

THERE HAVE BEEN MANY RECIPES for bread pudding in the "By Request" column, and requests for more keep coming in. What sets this recipe worlds apart from others is the Warm Whiskey Sauce that accompanies it. You will love it.

> ½ cup raisins
> 1 cup warm water
> ½ loaf French bread, cut into 1-inch cubes
> 1 quart half-and-half
> 4 eggs, beaten
> ¼ cup sugar
> 2 teaspoons vanilla extract
> Pinch of nutmeg
> ½ cup (1 stick) butter, melted
> Warm Whiskey Sauce (recipe follows)

Soak raisins in 1 cup warm water for 30 minutes, then drain. Lightly grease an 8-inch-square pan and fill with French bread cubes. (Use enough bread to come all the way to the top of the pan.) Sprinkle raisins on top.

Preheat oven to 325 degrees.

In a large bowl, whisk together the half-and-half, eggs, sugar, vanilla, nutmeg, and butter. Pour over the bread and raisins and lightly fold in using a spatula. (The pan will be very full. If you have too much batter, discard the excess. If there's not enough to fill the pan, add a little milk.) Allow the bread to soak for 30 minutes.

Bake for about 45 minutes, until the pudding is golden brown and puffed up around the edges. The center should be set but still a little soft. Serve with Warm Whiskey Sauce.

SERVES 8

WARM WHISKEY SAUCE

4 eggs, beaten
¼ cup whiskey
1 cup (2 sticks) butter
2 cups sugar

Using an electric mixer set at medium-low speed, in a small bowl, beat together eggs and whiskey. Set aside.

Melt butter in a large saucepan over low heat. Add the sugar and stir well. Remove from heat, let cool slightly, then quickly whisk in the beaten eggs and whiskey. Return the sauce to low heat on the stove and whisk constantly until the sauce has thickened slightly, about 6 to 8 minutes. (Overcooking will curdle the sauce.) Keep warm.

Approximate values per serving: 876 calories, 54 grams fat, 350 milligrams cholesterol, 84 grams carbohydrate, 635 milligrams sodium, 56 percent of calories from fat.

BUTTERMILK-CRUSTED BLACKBERRY COBBLER

The Weather Vane
MESA, ARIZONA

BLACKBERRY LOVERS can indulge their passion with this scrumptious dessert. Its wonderful aroma will entice you to go beyond one serving. This cobbler is even more tempting when topped with a premium vanilla ice cream.

FILLING

1½ pounds blackberries

1⅓ cups sugar

3½ tablespoons flour

1⅓ tablespoons vanilla extract

Grease an 8 x 12 x 8-inch pan.

In a medium bowl, combine blackberries, sugar, flour, and vanilla. Pour into greased pan.

CRUST

1 tablespoon plus 2½ teaspoons sugar

¾ teaspoon baking powder

¼ teaspoon salt

⅓ cup shortening

½ cup buttermilk

1⅓ cups flour

½ tablespoon melted butter

Preheat oven to 350 degrees.

In a large bowl, stir together 1 tablespoon of the sugar, baking powder, salt, shortening, buttermilk, and ¾ cup of the flour to form a sticky dough. Spread remaining flour on a work surface and knead dough until most of the flour is incorporated and dough is manageable. Roll dough to about ¼-inch thickness and cut with a knife into large pieces. Cover blackberry filling with dough, overlapping pieces. Drizzle melted butter over dough and sprinkle with remaining 2½ teaspoons of sugar.

Bake until crust is golden brown and filling is bubbly, about 50 minutes.

SERVES 8 TO 10

Approximate values per serving (based on 8 servings): 345 calories, 10 grams fat, 2 milligrams cholesterol, 63 grams carbohydrate, 114 milligrams sodium, 25 percent of calories from fat.

DOUBLE FUDGE NUT BROWNIES

Embassy Suites Hotel
SCOTTSDALE, ARIZONA

Carole Silverman, Food and Beverage Director

WHEN'S THE LAST TIME YOU MADE BROWNIES from scratch? What an incredible difference you'll taste when you make these! Try them topped with vanilla ice cream.

> *6 tablespoons margarine*
> *6 tablespoons butter*
> *½ cup unsweetened cocoa*
> *2 eggs*
> *1½ cups sugar*
> *⅔ cup bread flour*
> *½ cup walnuts, chopped*
> *Powdered sugar for garnish*

Preheat oven to 350 degrees. Grease and flour a 9 x 9-inch pan and set aside.

Melt margarine and butter together in a small saucepan. Add cocoa and stir until dissolved. Remove from heat and set aside.

Using an electric mixer set on medium speed, in a large mixing bowl, beat eggs and sugar together until smooth, about 2 to 3 minutes. Slowly add flour. Add cocoa mixture, combining well. Stir in chopped walnuts.

Pour into prepared pan and bake for 30 to 40 minutes, until tester comes out clean. When cool, dust with powdered sugar and cut into 3-inch squares.

MAKES 9 BROWNIES

Approximate values per serving: 373 calories, 21 grams fat, 77 milligrams cholesterol, 44 grams carbohydrate, 184 milligrams sodium, 49 percent of calories from fat.

PLUM TART

Capers Restaurant at the Orange Tree Golf
and Conference Resort

SCOTTSDALE, ARIZONA

Michael Janes, Pastry Chef

THIS UNUSUAL CHOCOLATE delicacy is as appealing to the eye as
it is to the taste buds.

CHOCOLATE SHELL

> *1 cup (2 sticks) butter*
> *½ cup sugar*
> *2 eggs*
> *½ teaspoon baking powder*
> *1 cup flour*
> *1 cup unsweetened cocoa powder*
> *Filling (recipe follows)*
> *5 plums for garnish*
> *½ cup apricot jam for garnish*

Using an electric mixer set at medium speed, in a large mixing
bowl, cream together the butter and the sugar. Add the eggs, using a
spatula to scrape the sides of the bowl. In a medium bowl, combine
the baking powder, flour, and cocoa. Slowly add the dry ingredients to
the butter-sugar mixture, blending well.

On a floured surface, roll the dough out to ¼-inch thickness.
Lightly grease a 9-inch tart mold or pie pan. Form the dough into the
pan and all the way up the sides. Cut away excess dough from the
edge. Chill in the refrigerator to set while preparing the filling.

Preheat oven to 325 degrees.

Spread filling into the chocolate shell and smooth flat with a
spatula.

Slice the plums in half and remove the pits. Slice each plum in half and lengthwise into fifths.

Arrange plum slices in a circular pattern on top of filling, pushing them in slightly. Cover filling completely with slices.

Bake at 325 degrees for 15 minutes, then lower the temperature to 300 degrees and continue baking for about 30 minutes or until tart is firm in the center.

Chill tart in the refrigerator until cool and firm. While tart is cooling, warm the apricot glaze.

Remove tart from pan and brush with warm apricot glaze. Cool slightly, then slice and serve at room temperature.

FILLING

> ½ cup (1 stick) butter
> ½ cup sugar
> 8 ounces (1 cup) almond paste
> ¼ cup oil
> 1 tablespoon crème de cacao liqueur
> ¼ cup puréed plums (or prepared puréed baby-food plums
>   without tapioca)
> 4 eggs
> 2 cups flour
> 1⅓ cups unsweetened cocoa

In a large mixing bowl, using an electric mixer set at medium speed, cream the butter, sugar, and almond paste together until smooth, about 3 minutes. Add the oil, crème de cacao, and puréed plums. Add eggs, mixing and scraping the bowl. In a medium mixing bowl, sift together the flour and cocoa. Add the dry ingredients to the butter-sugar mixture and mix to blend.

SERVES 12

Approximate values per serving: 712 calories, 39 grams fat, 155 milligrams cholesterol, 80 grams carbohydrate, 300 milligrams sodium, 49 percent of calories from fat.

Oatmeal Raisin Cookies

The Bakery Cafe at the Boulders Resort

CAREFREE, ARIZONA

Mary Nearn, Executive Chef

THESE GRAND COOKIES bring out the children in all of us.

1¼ cups (2½ sticks) butter

½ cup sugar

1⅛ cups brown sugar

1 egg

1 teaspoon vanilla extract

2 cups flour

1 teaspoon baking soda

¾ teaspoon salt

1 teaspoon ground cinnamon

¼ teaspoon ground nutmeg

2½ cups rolled oats

1 cup dark raisins

Preheat oven to 350 degrees.

Using an electric mixer set at medium speed, in a large mixing bowl, cream together butter and sugars. Add egg while scraping the bowl with a rubber spatula. Add vanilla. Sift together the flour, baking soda, salt, cinnamon, and nutmeg, and add slowly to the sugar mixture. Stir in oats and raisins.

Use an ice cream scoop to shape dough into balls and place 3 inches apart on a greased cookie sheet. Press each down lightly and bake 12 to 15 minutes or until cookies are golden brown.

MAKES 15 GIANT OR 3 DOZEN REGULAR COOKIES

Approximate values per cookie: 400 calories, 18 grams fat, 56 milligrams cholesterol, 56 grams carbohydrate, 368 milligrams sodium, 39 percent of calories from fat.

CARROT CAKE

The Sandolo Restaurant at the Hyatt Regency Scottsdale at Gainey Ranch

SCOTTSDALE, ARIZONA

Anton Brunbauer, Executive Chef

A FAVORITE OF MANY, this carrot cake is always welcome and always good—especially with the heavenly cream cheese frosting.

1¼ cups oil
1⅔ cups sugar
2 cups flour
2 teaspoons baking powder
1 teaspoon salt
1 teaspoon cinnamon
3 eggs
2 medium carrots, grated
1 cup chopped pecans
Cream Cheese Frosting (recipe follows)

Preheat oven to 350 degrees. Grease and flour a 9-inch cake pan.

Combine oil and sugar in a large mixing bowl and beat well. Sift together flour, baking powder, salt, and cinnamon in a separate bowl. Slowly add dry ingredients to the oil-sugar mixture, blending well. Add eggs, one at a time, mixing well after each addition. Stir in carrots and pecans.

Pour into prepared cake pan and bake for 45 to 50 minutes, or until a toothpick inserted in the center comes out clean. Cool before frosting.

SERVES 10

CREAM CHEESE FROSTING

> ½ cup (1 stick) unsalted butter, softened
> 1½ cups powdered sugar
> 12 ounces cream cheese

In a medium mixing bowl, cream together butter and powdered sugar. Add cream cheese and mix until perfectly smooth.

MAKES ABOUT 1¼ CUPS

Approximate values per serving: 837 calories, 58 grams fat, 127 milligrams cholesterol,
75 grams carbohydrate, 413 milligrams sodium, 61 percent of calories from fat.

UPROARIN' SONORAN
FRIED ICE CREAM

Macayo's Mexican Restaurant

PHOENIX AND SCOTTSDALE, ARIZONA

Mike Leitner, Corporate Chef

TAKE YOUR NEXT CELEBRATION over the top with this festive
dessert. Use coffee or vanilla ice cream and let your guests pile on their
favorite toppings. Kids will enjoy helping prepare this special treat.

> 1 cup sugar
> 3 tablespoons ground cinnamon
> 9 ounces cornflakes (one-half of an 18-ounce box)
> 1 quart vanilla or coffee ice cream
> Canola oil for frying
> Tortilla Dessert Shells (recipe follows)
> 1 cup honey, hot fudge, and/or sliced strawberries (fresh or
>   frozen and thawed)
> Whipped cream for garnish

Mix together sugar and cinnamon in a shallow pan. Place the cornflakes in a large bowl. Using an ice cream scoop, divide the ice cream into 8 portions and form each into a ball. Roll the ice cream balls in the sugar and cinnamon mixture to coat them evenly, being sure to maintain the roundness of each ball. Next, roll the balls in the cornflakes to coat them evenly. Place coated ice cream balls in a 9 x 13-inch pan and freeze for 1 hour or until hard.

Heat canola oil to 350 or 400 degrees in a deep fryer. Make sure fryer has reached proper temperature so balls will brown quickly.

Remove the hardened ice cream balls from the freezer and deep fry them for 3 seconds each, or until the cornflake coating has browned. After frying, allow the balls to drain completely on paper towels.

Place each prepared Tortilla Dessert Shell on a small plate and set an ice cream ball into the shell. Pour 2 tablespoons of honey, hot fudge, or strawberries on top. Pipe the whipped cream around and on top of each ice cream ball, forming 5 rosettes. Serve immediately.

SERVES 8

TORTILLA DESSERT SHELLS

Eight 8-inch flour tortillas
Canola oil for deep frying

Place each tortilla around a tortilla basket mold and deep fry in hot canola oil for 1 minute or until golden brown. Drain the cooked shell on a paper towel. Do not refrigerate.

NOTE: *If a tortilla basket mold is not available, use tongs to carefully push down the center of the tortilla while it is frying.*

Approximate values per serving: 737 calories, 29 grams fat, 49 milligrams cholesterol, 115 grams carbohydrate, 554 milligrams sodium, 35 percent of calories from fat.

FINANCIER

Pierre's Pastry Café

SCOTTSDALE, ARIZONA

Pierre Fauvet, chef/owner

ONE OF MY FAVORITE PASTRIES is a muffinlike goody called "Financier." Butter is the essence of this mouth-watering recipe. Be sure you heat yours until amber in color.

3¼ cups powdered sugar
1½ cups almond flour
1½ cups flour
1 tablespoon baking powder
1 teaspoon salt
1½ cups (3 sticks) unsalted butter
2⅛ cups egg whites (about 9)
2¼ teaspoons vanilla extract

In a large mixing bowl, mix together powdered sugar, almond flour, flour, baking powder, and salt.

Brown butter in a small saucepan on high heat until amber in color. Add butter to flour mixture and mix well using an electric mixer set at medium speed. Add egg whites and vanilla, scraping down bowl with a spatula. Mixture will be soupy. Chill overnight in the refrigerator.

The next day, preheat oven to 375 degrees. Grease 18 muffin tins. Using an ice cream scoop, fill muffin tins three-quarters full. Bake for 25 minutes.

SERVES 18

NOTE: *If almond flour is unavailable, process slivered almonds in a food processor until fine.*

Approximate values per serving: 261 calories, 21 grams fat, 41 milligrams cholesterol, 13 grams carbohydrate, 235 milligrams sodium, 71 percent of calories from fat.

CHOCOLATE ENCHILADAS

The Compass at the Hyatt Regency Phoenix

PHOENIX, ARIZONA

Jeffrey Axell, Executive Chef

MANY "SNOWBIRDS" ESCAPE the northern cold by enjoying the desert sun and dining on this enticing treat. It is very rich, very good, and very chocolate.

> *8 ounces bittersweet chocolate squares*
> *½ cup heavy cream*
> *6 chocolate crepes*
> *1½ cups whipping cream*
> *3 ounces hazelnuts, chopped*
> *3 ounces milk chocolate shavings*
> *3 ounces white chocolate shavings*
> *1 teaspoon cinnamon*
> *1 cup vanilla gelato, melted*
> *½ cup fresh berries*

Melt bittersweet chocolate squares in a heavy saucepan over very low heat. Stir constantly until just melted, then stir in heavy cream. Using a pastry brush, coat one side of each crepe with this chocolate "ganache." Place crepes on wax paper, ganache side up, and place in the refrigerator until ready to use.

With an electric mixer set at medium-high speed, in a medium mixing bowl, whip the whipping cream until firm but not stiff. Fold in the hazelnuts and almost all of the chocolate shavings, reserving some white chocolate shavings for garnish. Place this cream mixture into a pastry bag. Place the chocolate crepes, ganache side down, on wax paper. Pipe approximately ¼ cup of the cream mixture in a line down the center of each crepe and roll to close.

In a small bowl, stir the cinnamon into the melted gelato.

Spoon 2 to 3 tablespoons onto a plate, place chocolate enchilada on top and spoon fresh berries over the enchilada. Sprinkle with white chocolate shavings.

SERVES 6

NOTE: *Chocolate crepes and gelato can be found in the frozen foods section of well-stocked grocery stores.*

Approximate values per serving: 720 calories, 55 grams fat, 117 milligrams cholesterol, 56 grams carbohydrate, 301 milligrams sodium, 66 percent of calories from fat.

PRALINE CHEESECAKE

Z'Tejas Grill

SCOTTSDALE, ARIZONA

Leo Madrigal, Chef

THERE ISN'T A DESSERT more elegant than a superb cheesecake, and this recipe takes top honors. It is very rich but not too heavy.

1½ cups graham cracker crumbs
2 tablespoons plus 2 teaspoons granulated sugar
2 tablespoons plus 2 teaspoons margarine, melted

Grease and line a ten-inch springform pan with parchment paper. Mix all crust ingredients together in a small mixing bowl. Using 1½ cups of crumbs, spoon or pat a thin layer over the bottom of the pan.

Pour filling (recipe follows) into crust.

Bake for two hours. Let cool.

Pour topping (recipe follows) over cooled cheesecake, slice, and serve.

SERVES 6 TO 8

FILLING

> 2 cups plus 4 teaspoons cream cheese
>
> 1⅔ cups sugar
>
> ½ teaspoon vanilla extract
>
> 5 eggs
>
> 2 tablespoons plus 2 teaspoons Frangelico liqueur
>
> 1 cup pecan pieces

Preheat oven to 200 degrees.

Using an electric mixer, in a large mixing bowl, beat together cream cheese and sugar. Add vanilla. Continue to beat while scraping the sides of the bowl with a spatula. Add eggs slowly, one at a time, and continue to beat. Mix in liqueur and pecans.

NOTE: *This recipe calls for very low heat, which yields a moist, fluffy cheesecake. When I made it at home, it took longer than 2 hours for the cheesecake to bake completely. Chef Madrigal suggests increasing the temperature slightly to 225 degrees for a shorter baking time.*

TOPPING

> ⅓ cup sugar
>
> ⅓ cup brown sugar
>
> 1 tablespoon plus 1 teaspoon light Karo syrup
>
> 2 tablespoons plus 2 teaspoons milk
>
> Pinch of salt
>
> ⅔ cup pecans
>
> 2 tablespoons butter
>
> 1 teaspoon vanilla extract

Combine the sugars, syrup, milk, and salt in a medium saucepan. Cook over medium heat, until sugars are dissolved and mixture begins to boil. Remove from heat and stir in the pecans, butter, and vanilla. Mix together.

Approximate values per serving (based on 8): 808 calories, 48 grams fat, 206 milligrams cholesterol, 86 grams carbohydrate, 481 milligrams sodium, 52 percent of calories from fat.

RUSTIC PEAR PIE

Nola's Mexican Restaurant
PHOENIX, ARIZONA

Melinda Bugarin, Chef

THIS IS A UNIQUE DESSERT. Although one of these small empanadas is really meant to serve two, you may find them very difficult to share.

> 2⅔ cups flour, sifted
> ⅓ cup sugar
> 1⅓ cups (2 sticks, 5 tablespoons, and 1 teaspoon) butter, cold
> 3 tablespoons water
> 2 teaspoons vanilla extract

In a large mixing bowl, stir together flour and sugar. Add butter slowly, mixing well. Add water and vanilla, then mix on medium speed with an electric mixer for 3 minutes.

Preheat oven to 350 degrees. Grease a sheet pan.

Form dough into eight 5-inch circles on sheet pan. Place pear filling (recipe follows) in the middle of each dough square. Pinch edges up to keep filling in and top with Streusel (recipe follows). Bake for 40 to 50 minutes, until golden brown.

MAKES 8 INDIVIDUAL PIES, 2 SERVINGS PER PIE

FILLING

> 4 pears, peeled, cored, and chopped
> 3 tablespoons sugar
> 1 tablespoon plus 1 teaspoon brown sugar
> ⅛ teaspoon ground cinnamon
> ⅛ teaspoon ground nutmeg

⅛ teaspoon ground ginger

1 vanilla bean

Combine all filling ingredients in a small saucepan. Cook over medium heat for 3 minutes or until warm. Remove vanilla bean.

STREUSEL

2⅔ cups flour

1 cup sugar

½ teaspoon ground cinnamon

32 tablespoons (2 cups) cold butter, sliced

Mix together flour, sugar, and cinnamon in a medium bowl. Add butter and stir to cover.

Approximate values per serving: 593 calories, 39 grams fat, 104 milligrams cholesterol, 58 grams carbohydrate, 392 milligrams sodium, 58 percent of calories from fat.

PECAN BAR COOKIES

The Bakery Cafe at The Boulders Resort

CAREFREE, ARIZONA

Mary Nearn, Executive Chef

THE AROMA OF THESE bar cookies will make your mouth water. These delicious little cookies won't last long.

CRUST

1¼ cups (2½ sticks) unsalted butter

¾ cup granulated sugar

2 tablespoons heavy cream

2 egg yolks

3½ cups flour
Pecan Filling (recipe follows)

Preheat oven to 325 degrees. Lightly grease a 10 x 15-inch sheet pan; set aside.

Using an electric mixer, in a large mixing bowl, cream together the butter and sugar until smooth. Add heavy cream and egg yolks, mixing until smooth. Slowly add flour, mixing until just incorporated. Do not overmix. Press into the prepared sheet pan and bake for 8 to 10 minutes until barely golden. Let cool.

Preheat oven to 325 degrees.

Pour filling into prebaked shell. Bake for 20 to 25 minutes until bubbling on top. Cool and cut into 1½-inch squares.

MAKES ABOUT 60 SQUARES

PECAN FILLING

½ cup (1 stick) unsalted butter
1 cup brown sugar
¼ cup sugar
⅓ cup honey
⅛ cup heavy cream
2¾ cups pecan pieces, lightly toasted

In a medium saucepan, melt together the butter, sugars, and honey. Bring to a boil and boil for 3 minutes. Stir in heavy cream and remove from heat. Stir in pecans.

Approximate values per serving: 143 calories, 10 grams fat, 24 milligrams cholesterol, 14 grams carbohydrate, 3 milligrams sodium, 60 percent of calories from fat.

KEY LIME PIE

The Chart House

SCOTTSDALE, ARIZONA

Karen Bede, Executive Chef

KEY LIME PIE has always been a favorite summer dessert for my family. No matter what we eat for dinner, we always leave room for a slice (or two) of this tart treat. I thought I had tasted the best until I tried this delicious version.

> 1⅓ cups graham cracker crumbs
> ½ cup (1 stick) butter, melted
> Nonstick cooking spray
> 6 egg yolks
> 2 cans (14 ounces each) condensed milk
> ¾ teaspoon cream of tartar
> ¾ cup Key lime juice

In a medium bowl, stir together the graham cracker crumbs and melted butter until well blended. Lightly grease a 9-inch pie plate with nonstick cooking spray, then spread the crust mixture evenly (about ½ inch thick) over the bottom and sides of the pie plate. Set aside.

Preheat oven to 325 degrees.

In a large mixing bowl, beat egg yolks with an electric mixer until foamy, about 3 minutes. Add condensed milk and cream of tartar and blend on low speed for about 1 minute. Pour in the Key lime juice and mix for 1 minute more. Ladle this mixture into the prepared pie shell. The liquid should reach the top of the crust.

Place pie on a sheet pan and bake for 12 minutes. The color should be light yellow, with a smooth, creamy consistency. Cool for 15 minutes at room temperature, then place in the freezer until ready to serve.

SERVES 6

Approximate values per serving: 737 calories, 34 grams fat, 367 milligrams cholesterol, 94 grams carbohydrate, 439 milligrams sodium, 41 percent of calories from fat.

OREO CAKE

Tomatoes

SCOTTSDALE, ARIZONA

Karen Crouse, Pastry Chef

THIS SINFULLY DELICIOUS CAKE is fun to make, and even more fun to eat.

CAKE

> *2 cups cake flour*
> *1 teaspoon baking soda*
> *½ teaspoon salt*
> *6 tablespoons unsweetened cocoa*
> *½ cup (1 stick) butter, softened*
> *1 teaspoon vanilla extract*
> *1¼ cups sugar*
> *2 eggs*
> *1 cup milk*
> *1 one-pound package Oreo cookies, crushed*
> *Icing (recipe follows)*

Preheat oven to 350 degrees. Butter and flour two 8-inch round cake pans.

Sift together flour, baking soda, salt, and cocoa. In a large mixing bowl, using an electric mixer set at medium speed, cream butter. Add vanilla and sugar and beat well. Add eggs one at a time, scraping the bowl with a rubber spatula and beating well after each addition. Add the sifted dry ingredients in three additions alternating with the milk in two additions. Beat on low speed after each addition, only until smooth.

Pour batter evenly into the cake pans and bake for 35 to 40 minutes or until cake comes away from the sides of the pan. Remove and let cool. Wrap in plastic wrap and refrigerate until ready to ice.

Place one cake round upside down on a flat plate. (You may need to cut off the top part of the cake if it baked unevenly.) Spread a generous amount of icing on top of the cake. Add some of the crushed cookies, pressing them into the icing. Place the other cake round, flat side up, on top of the cookies. Smooth a generous amount of icing on the top and sides of the cake. Press crushed cookies over entire surface of cake.

SERVES 10 TO 12

ICING

> 1 cup (2 sticks) butter
> 1 cup cream cheese
> 7½ cups powdered sugar
> 2 teaspoons vanilla extract
> 1 one-pound package Oreo cookies, crushed

Using an electric mixer, cream butter and cream cheese together until soft and free of lumps, scraping the bowl often. Sift the powdered sugar and add slowly to the butter-cream cheese mixture, scraping the bowl often. Add the vanilla and mix on medium speed for 1 minute, thoroughly blending the icing until smooth.

Approximate values per serving (based on 12): 862 calories, 40 grams fat, 119 milligrams cholesterol, 139 grams carbohydrate, 755 milligrams sodium, 41 percent of calories from fat.

RUM CAKE

Pischke's Paradise
SCOTTSDALE, ARIZONA

Betty Stewart Pischke

MANY HAVE ENJOYED this wonderful cake.

1 box (18.25 ounces) Betty Crocker yellow cake mix
1 box (3.4-ounces) vanilla Jell-O instant pudding mix
½ cup vegetable oil
½ cup water
½ cup dark rum
4 eggs
Glaze (recipe follows)

Preheat oven to 350 degrees. Grease and flour a Bundt pan.

With an electric mixer set on high speed, in a large mixing bowl, combine cake mix, pudding mix, oil, water, rum, and eggs and blend on high speed for 2 to 3 minutes.

Pour into Bundt pan and bake for 45 minutes. Turn out onto a 9-inch pie plate (with a lip) immediately upon removal from the oven. When cake is nearly cool, poke holes all over (inside, outside, sides, and top) using a fork. Pour glaze over cake.

SERVES 8 GENEROUSLY

GLAZE

¼ cup water
½ cup (1 stick) butter
1 cup sugar
½ cup dark rum

In a small saucepan, heat water and butter over medium heat. When butter melts, add sugar and stir. Boil for 5 minutes, stirring constantly. Remove from heat and stir in rum.

Approximate values per serving: 743 calories, 35 grams fat, 138 milligrams cholesterol, 87 grams carbohydrate, 747 mg sodium, 46 percent of calories from fat.

BLACKBERRY CINNAMON BREAD PUDDING

Mulligan's Steak and Seafood
SCOTTSDALE AND GILBERT, ARIZONA

THIS SCRUMPTIOUS PUDDING makes a perfect summertime treat. Every bite has an abundance of sweet blackberries kissed with cinnamon.

4 eggs, lightly beaten
1¼ cups sugar
1 tablespoon vanilla extract
2 cups half-and-half
1 cup milk
1 tablespoon ground cinnamon
1 loaf white bread, crusts removed, cut into bite-size pieces
4 cups fresh blackberries
Glaze (recipe follows)

Preheat oven to 350 degrees. Lightly grease a 9 x 13-inch pan.

In a medium bowl, combine the eggs, ¾ cup of the sugar, and vanilla, stirring well. Add the half-and-half and milk and stir to combine. Set aside.

In a small bowl, combine remaining ½ cup sugar and cinnamon. Place one layer of bread pieces on the bottom of the prepared pan. Top with a layer of fresh blackberries and sprinkle with sugar-cinnamon mixture. Repeat this procedure three times, ending with a layer of bread on top. Pour custard mixture over, allowing to soak through the layers. Bake until golden brown, about 45 to 50 minutes. Top with glaze and serve.

SERVES 16

GLAZE

> *7 egg yolks, lightly beaten*
> *1 cup sugar*
> *2 cups heavy cream*
> *½ tablespoon vanilla extract*

Combine the egg yolks and sugar in a double boiler over medium-high heat. Slowly stir in the heavy cream and stir constantly until it begins to thicken, about 5 minutes. Let cool and stir in vanilla.

Approximate values per serving: 370 calories, 19 grams fat, 193 milligrams cholesterol, 42 grams carbohydrate, 7 grams protein, 182 milligrams sodium, 47 percent of calories from fat.

GLOSSARY OF TERMS

Al dente: An Italian term describing the consistency of pasta cooked to a tender firmness, usually considered to be "just right."

Deglaze: To create a gravy by heating stock or wine in a pan in which meat or vegetables have cooked. Stir vigorously to loosen particles and residue that may be stuck to the pan.

Demi-glace: A basic French sauce made with meat stock and roux and reduced in volume to between one-half and one-tenth by boiling.

Dredge: To lightly cover food with flour, cornmeal, or bread crumbs.

Egg Wash: A lightly beaten egg diluted with water or milk, used to give gloss and color to a dough or pastry.

Flambé: To set a match to a food flavored with brandy or liqueur.

Ganache: An extremely rich butter cream (usually chocolate or mocha) used for filling pastries, tarts, etc.

Masa: A coarsely ground corn flour used to make tortillas, tamales, and other dishes.

Panko Bread Crumbs: A Japanese-style bread crumb used in many recipes.

Poblano: A small, mild chile pepper with a dark green color and pleasant taste; common in Southwestern dishes.

Prosciutto: Cured ham.

Roux: Flour browned carefully in fat, butter, or oil, or mixed with water or stock; used to thicken and season gravies, sauces, and soups.

Sear: To seal in the juices of a cut of meat by browning it rapidly at high heat in a skillet or in the oven.

Sweat: Heating or sautéeing onions until just translucent.

Tournedos: Small fillets of tenderloin.

CONTRIBUTING RESTAURANTS

The Arizona Club is located at 201 N. Central Avenue in Phoenix and at 7150 E. Camelback Road in Scottsdale.

Aunt Pittypat's Pantry is located at 7123 N. 58th Avenue in Glendale. Phoenix and 3102 N. Scottsdale Road in Scottsdale.

Baby Kay's is located at 7216 Shoeman Lane in Scottsdale and 2119 E. Camelback Road in Phoenix.

The Bakery Cafe at the Boulders Resort is located at 34505 N. Scottsdale Road in Carefree.

The Bamboo Club is located at 2596 E. Camelback Road in the Biltmore Fashion Park, Phoenix, and at 8624 E. Shea Boulevard, Scottsdale.

The Bean Tree Coffee House is located at 7818 N. 12th Street in Phoenix.

The Beaver Street Brewery and Whistle Stop Cafe is located at 11 S. Beaver Street in historic downtown Flagstaff.

Beeloe's Cafe is located at 501 S. Mill Avenue in Tempe.

The Biltmore Grill at the Arizona Biltmore is located at 24th Street and Missouri Avenue in Phoenix.

Bola's Grill at the Holiday Inn Old Town Scottsdale is located at 7353 E. Indian School Road in Scottsdale.

Cantina del Pedregal is located at 34631 N. Tom Darlington Drive in Carefree.

Capers Restaurant at the Orange Tree Golf and Conference Resort is located at 10601 N. 56th Street in Scottsdale.

Casey Moore's Oyster House is located at 850 S. Ash Avenue in Tempe.

The Chart House is located at 7255 E. McCormick Parkway in Scottsdale.

Chevy's Mexican Restaurant is located at 2650 E. Camelback Road in Phoenix and other locations.

Christopher's Bistro is located at 2398 E. Camelback Road in Phoenix.

The Compass at the Hyatt Regency Phoenix is located at 122 N. Second Street in Phoenix.

Cork 'N Cleaver is located at 5101 N. 44th Street in Phoenix.

The Country Glazed Ham Company is located at 6045 N. Scottsdale Road in Scottsdale.

The Coyote Grill is located at 3202 E. Greenway Road in Phoenix.

Cucina! Cucina! Italian Cafe is located at 12031 N. Tatum Boulevard in Paradise Valley, 4921 E. Ray Road in Ahwatukee, and 2501 E. Camelback Road in Phoenix.

Eddie's Grill is located at 4747 N. Seventh Street in Phoenix.

The El Tovar Hotel is located right on the canyon rim in the historic section of Grand Canyon Village.

The Embassy Suites Hotel is located at 5001 N. Scottsdale Road, Scottsdale.

The Fish Market is located at 1720 E. Camelback Road in Phoenix.

Franco's Trattoria is located at 8120 N. Hayden Road in Scottsdale.

Fuego Restaurant at the Doubletree Paradise Valley Resort is located at 5401 N. Scottsdale Road, Scottsdale.

The Good Egg is located at 906 E. Camelback Road, Phoenix, and other locations in the Phoenix area.

Gooseberries is located at 15414 N. Seventh Street in Phoenix.

The Grand Cafe is located at 1119 G Avenue in Douglas.

Greektown is located at the southwest corner of 7th Street and Glendale Avenue in Phoenix.

Harvey's Wineburgers is located at 4812 N. 16th Street in Phoenix.

Havana Café is located at 6245 E. Bell Road in Scottsdale and 4225 E. Camelback Road in Phoenix.

Hops! Bistro and Brewery is located at 2566 E. Camelback Road in the Biltmore Fashion Park, Phoenix, and at 6900 E. Camelback Road in Scottsdale Fashion Square, Scottsdale.

The Hyatt Regency Scottsdale at Gainey Ranch is located at 7500 E. Doubletree Ranch Road in Scottsdale.

Kohnie's Gourmet Coffee is located at 4233 E. Camelback Road in Phoenix.

La Mediterraneé de Sedona was located on Highway 179 in Sedona, but sadly is now closed.

Macayo's Mexican Restaurant is located at 4001 N. Central Avenue, Phoenix, and other locations throughout the Valley.

Malee's on Main is located at 7131 E. Main Street in Scottsdale.

Maria's When In Naples is located at 7000 E. Shea Boulevard in Scottsdale.

Mimi's Cafe is located at 8980 E. Shea Boulevard in Scottsdale.

NM Cafe at Neiman Marcus is located in Scottsdale Fashion Square, 7014 E. Camelback Road, Scottsdale.

Nola's Mexican Restaurant is located at 2566 E. Camelback Road at the Biltmore Fashion Park, Phoenix.

Old Town Tortilla Factory is located at 6910 E. Main in Old Town Scottsdale.

The Phoenician is located at 6000 E. Camelback Road in Scottsdale.

Pierre's Pastry Café is located at 7119 E. Shea Boulevard, Suite 100, in Scottsdale.

Pischke's Paradise is located at 7217 E. First Street and 7000 E. Shea Boulevard in Scottsdale.

Planet Hollywood is located at 2402 E. Camelback Road in Phoenix.

Players Sports Bar is located at the Arizona Center, 455 N. Third Street, Phoenix.

Prescott Brewing Company is located at 130 W. Gurley Street in Prescott.

Razz's Restaurant and Bar is located at 10321 N. Scottsdale Road in Scottsdale.

Richardson's is located at 1582 E. Bethany Home Road in Phoenix.

RoxSand Restaurant and Bar is located at 2594 E. Camelback Road in Phoenix.

Sam's Cafe is located at the Arizona Center, 455 N. Third Street and also at 2566 E. Camelback Road in the Biltmore Fashion Park, both in Phoenix.

Sandolo Restaurant at the Hyatt Regency Scottsdale at Gainey Ranch is located at 7500 E. Doubletree Ranch Road in Scottsdale.

Sfuzzi is located at 4720 N. Scottsdale Road in Scottsdale and at the Arrowhead Towne Center in Glendale.

Sorrento's Italian Kitchen is located at 832 W. Baseline Road in Tempe and 2111 E. Main Street in Mesa.

The Spicery is located at 7141 N. 59th Avenue in Glendale.

Sprouts Restaurant at Marriott's Camelback Inn Resort is located at 5402 E. Lincoln Drive in Scottsdale.

The Teacup Dining Room at the Hassayampa Inn is located at 122 E. Gurley in Prescott.

The Terrace Dining Room at the Wigwam Resort is located at 300 E. Wigwam Boulevard in Litchfield Park.

Tomatoes is located at 7014 E. Camelback Road at the Scottsdale Fashion Square, Scottsdale.

Treet's Deli at A. J.'s Fine Foods is located at 5017 N. Central Avenue in Phoenix.

Ventanas at the Scottsdale Princess Resort is located at 7575 E. Princess Drive in Scottsdale.

Vincent Guerithault on Camelback is located at 3930 E. Camelback Road in Phoenix.

The Vintage Market is located at 2442 E. Camelback Road in the Biltmore Fashion Park, Phoenix.

The Weather Vane is located at 7303 E. Main Street in Mesa.

Windows on the Green at The Phoenician is located at 6000 E. Camelback Road in Scottsdale.

Z'Tejas Grill is located at 7014 E. Camelback Road in the Scottsdale Fashion Square, Scottsdale.

INDEX

BETSY MANN has been a weekly correspondent for *The Arizona Republic* since 1994. "By Request" draws from countless *Republic* readers seeking to prepare restaurant recipes at home. Also a freelance contributor to *The Houston Post, The Atlanta Journal-Constitution,* and *The Kansas City Star,* Betsy has a degree in food science and human nutrition from the University of Missouri.

The computer and kitchen occupy only part of Betsy's time at home. She and her husband, Dinn, have a four-year-old daughter, Caroline, and this year the Manns added twin daughters to their household. They have a cat, Pasta, and a dog, Romeo.